"ONE OF THE BEST, MOST DISTURBING, AND
MOST POWERFUL BOOKS ABOUT THE SHAME
THAT WAS/IS VIETNAM."
—*The Minneapolis Star and Tribune*

"ITS EFFECT IS AS DEVASTATING AS IF ITS AU-
THOR HAD BEEN KILLED. BUT HE SURVIVED. SO,
THROUGH SUCH WRITING, MAY THE AMERICAN
LANGUAGE." —*The Times* (London)

"A GENUINE MEMOIR IN THE FULL LITERARY
SENSE OF THAT TERM, and a work that quickly estab-
lished itself among Vietnam narratives as an exemplar of
the genre. . . . It recalls the depictions of men at war by
Whitman, Melville, Crane, and Hemingway; and it stands
at the same time in the central tradition of American
spiritual autobiography as well, the tradition of Edwards
and Woolman, of Franklin and Thoreau and Henry Adams."
—Philip D. Beidler, *American Literature
and the Experience of Vietnam*

"O'BRIEN WRITES WITH PAIN AND PASSION on the
nature of war and its effect on the men who fight in it. *If I
Die in a Combat Zone* may, in fact, be the single greatest
piece of work to come out of Vietnam, a work on a level
with World War Two's *The Naked and the Dead* and *From
Here to Eternity*." —*The Washington Star*

"O'BRIEN BRILLIANTLY AND QUIETLY EVOKES THE FOOT SOLDIER'S DAILY LIFE IN THE PADDIES AND FOXHOLES, EVOKES A BLIND, BLUNDERING WAR. . . . Tim O'Brien writes with the care and eloquence of someone for whom communication is still a vital possibility. . . . It is a beautiful, painful book, arousing pity and fear for the daily realities of a modern disaster."

—Annie Gottlieb, *The New York Times Book Review*

"WHAT ESPECIALLY DISTINGUISHES IT IS THE INTENSITY OF ITS SKETCHES FROM THE INFANTRY, AN INTENSITY SELDOM SEEN IN JOURNALISTIC ACCOUNTS OF THE WAR."

—Michael Casey, *America*

"AN ADMIRABLE BOOK BY AN ADMIRABLE MAN . . . a finely tuned, almost laconic account of soldiers at work." —*Playboy*

"A CONTROLLED, HONEST, WELL-WRITTEN ACCOUNT . . . MR. O'BRIEN IS EDUCATED, INTELLIGENT, REFLECTIVE, AND THOROUGHLY NICE— ALL QUALITIES THAT MAKE HIS A CONVINCING VOICE." —*The New Yorker*

"IT'S A TRUE WRITER'S JOB, GAINING STRENGTH BY DODGING THE RHETORIC, AND MUST BE ONE OF THE FEW GOOD THINGS TO COME OUT OF THAT DESOLATING STRUGGLE."

—*The Manchester Guardian*

Books by Tim O'Brien

IF I DIE IN A COMBAT ZONE

GOING AFTER CACCIATO

THE NUCLEAR AGE

IF I DIE IN A COMBAT ZONE

Box Me Up
And Ship Me Home

TIM O'BRIEN

FOR MY FAMILY

A LAUREL BOOK
Published by
Dell Publishing
a division of
Bantam Doubleday Dell Publishing Group, Inc.
1540 Broadway
New York, New York 10036

Portions of this book appeared in *Playboy* magazine, *The Washington Post*, *The Minneapolis Tribune*, and *Worthington Daily Globe*.

Excerpt from "Laches" from *The Dialogues of Plato* translated by Benjamin Jowett. Copyright © Clarendon Press, Oxford, 1953. Used by permission of the publisher.
Excerpt from "The Waste Land" from *Collected Poems 1909–1962* by T.S. Eliot. Used by permission of Harcourt Brace Jovanovich, Inc. and Faber and Faber Ltd.
Lines from "Homeward Bound" by Paul Simon. Copyright © 1966 by Paul Simon. Used by permission of Charing Cross Music, Inc.
Excerpt from "Hugh Selwyn Mauberly"—IV from *Persónae* by Ezra Pound. Copyright 1926 by Ezra Pound. Used by permission of New Directions Publishing Corporation and Faber and Faber Ltd.

ISBN: 0-440-34311-9

Reprinted by arrangement with Delacorte Press/Seymour Lawrence

Printed in the United States of America
Published simultaneously in Canada

June 1987

20 19 18

RAD

CONTENTS

lo maggior don che Dio per sua
larghezza / fesse creando . . . /
. . . fu de la volontà la libertate

THE DIVINE COMEDY
Par. V, 19 ff.

I

Days

"It's incredible, it really is, isn't it? Ever think you'd be humping along some crazy-ass trail like this, jumping up and down like a goddamn bullfrog, dodging bullets all day? Back in Cleveland, man, I'd still be asleep." Barney smiled. "You ever see anything like this? *Ever?*"

"Yesterday," I said.

"Yesterday? Shit, yesterday wasn't nothing like this."

"Snipers yesterday, snipers today. What's the difference?"

"Guess so." Barney shrugged. "Holes in your ass either way, right? But, I swear, yesterday wasn't *nothing* like this."

"Snipers yesterday, snipers today," I said again.

Barney laughed. "I tell you one thing," he said. "You think this is bad, just wait till tonight. My God, tonight'll be lovely. I'm digging me a foxhole like a basement."

We lay next to each other until the volley of fire stopped. We didn't bother to raise our rifles. We didn't know which way to shoot, and it was all over anyway.

Barney picked up his helmet and took out a pencil and put a mark on it. "See," he said, grinning and showing me ten marks, "that's ten times today. Count them—one, two, three, four, five, six, seven, eight, nine, *ten!* Ever been shot at ten times in one day?"

"Yesterday," I said. "And the day before that, and the day before that."

"No way. It's been lots worse today."

"Did you count yesterday?"

"No. Didn't think of it until today. That proves today's worse."

"Well, you should've counted yesterday."

We lay quietly for a time, waiting for the shooting to end, then Barney peeked up. "Off your ass, pal. Company's moving out." He put his pencil away and jumped up like a little kid on a pogo stick. Barney had heart.

I followed him up the trail, taking care to stay a few meters behind him. Barney was not one to worry about land mines. Or snipers. Or dying. He just didn't worry.

"You know," I said, "you really amaze me, kid. No kidding. This crap doesn't get you down, does it?"

"Can't *let* it," Barney said. "Know what I mean? That's how a man gets himself lethalized."

"Yeah, but—"

"You just can't *let* it get you down."

It was a hard march and soon enough we stopped the chatter. The day was hot. The days were always hot, even the cool days, and we concentrated on the heat and the fatigue and the simple motions of the march. It went that way for hours. One leg, the next leg. Legs counted the days.

"What time is it?"

"Don't know." Barney didn't look back at me. "Four o'clock maybe."

"Good."

"Tuckered? I'll hump some of that stuff for you, just give the word."

"No, it's okay. We should stop soon. I'll help you dig that basement."

"Cool."

"Basements, I like the sound. Cold, deep. Basements."

A shrill sound. A woman's shriek, a sizzle, a zipping-up sound. It was there, then it was gone, then it was there again.

"Jesus Christ almighty," Barney shouted. He was already flat on his belly. "You okay?"

"I guess. You?"

"No pain. They were *aiming* at us that time, I swear. You and me."

"Charlie knows who's after him," I said. "You and me."

Barney giggled. "Sure, we'd give 'em hell, wouldn't we? Strangle the little bastards."

We got up, brushed ourselves off, and continued along the line of march.

The trail linked a cluster of hamlets together, little villages to the north and west of the Batangan Peninsula. Dirty, tangled country. Empty villes. No people, no dogs or chickens. It was a fairly wide and flat trail, but it made dangerous slow curves and was flanked by deep hedges and brush. Two squads moved through the tangles on either side of us, protecting the flanks from close-in ambushes, and the company's progress was slow.

"Captain says we're gonna search one more ville today," Barney said. "Maybe—"

"What's he expect to find?"

Barney shrugged. He walked steadily and did not look back.

"Well, what *does* he expect to find? Charlie?"

"Who knows?"

"Get off it, man. Charlie finds *us*. All day long he's been shooting us up. How's that going to change?"

"Search me," Barney said. "Maybe we'll surprise him."

"Who?"

"Charlie. Maybe we'll surprise him this time."

"You kidding me, Barney?"

The kid giggled. "Can't never tell. I'm tired, so maybe ol' Charles is tired too. That's when we spring our little surprise."

"Tired," I muttered. "Wear the yellow bastards down, right?"

But Barney wasn't listening.

Soon the company stopped moving. Captain Johansen walked up to the front of the column, conferred with a lieutenant, then moved back. He asked for the radio handset, and I listened while he called battalion headquarters and told them we'd found the village and were about to cordon and search it. Then the platoons separated into their own little columns and began circling the hamlet that lay hidden behind thick brush. This was the bad time: The wait.

"What's the name of this goddamn place?" Barney said. He threw down his helmet and sat on it. "Funny, isn't it? Somebody's gonna ask me someday where the hell I was over here, where the bad action was, and, shit, what will I say?"

"Tell them St. Vith."

"What?"

"St. Vith," I said. "That's the name of this ville. It's right here on the map. Want to look?"

He grinned. "What's the difference? You say St. Vith, I guess that's it. I'll never remember. How

14

long's it gonna take me to forget *your* fuckin' name?"

The captain walked over and sat down with us, and together we smoked and waited for the platoons to fan out around the village. Now and then a radio would buzz. I handled the routine calls, Captain Johansen took everything important. All this was familiar: Cordon, wait, sweep, search. The mechanics were simple and sterile.

"This gonna take long?" Barney asked.

Captain Johansen said he hoped not. Hard to tell.

"What I mean is, you don't expect to find anything —right, sir?" Barney looked a little embarrassed. "That's what O'Brien was saying. Says it's hopeless. But like I told him, there's always the chance we can surprise old Charlie. Right? Always a *chance*."

The captain didn't answer.

I closed my eyes. Optimism always made me sleepy. We waited.

When the cordon was tied up tight, Barney and the captain and I joined the first platoon. Johansen gave the order to move in. And slowly, carefully, we tip-toed into the little hamlet, nudging over jugs of rice, watching where we walked, alert to booby traps, brains foggy, numb, hoping to find nothing.

But we found tunnels. Three of them. It was late afternoon now, and the men were tired, and issue was whether to search the tunnels or blow them.

"So," a lieutenant said. "Do we go down?"

The men murmured. One by one we moved away, leaving the lieutenant standing alone by the cluster of tunnels. He peered at them, kicked a little dirt into the mouths, then turned away.

He walked over to Captain Johansen and they had a short conference together. The sun was setting. Already it was impossible to make out the color in their faces and uniforms. The two officers stood together, heads down, deciding.

"Blow the fuckers up," someone said. "Right now, before they make up their minds. *Now*."

"Fire-in-the-hole!" Three explosions, dulled by dirt and sand, and the tunnels were blocked. *"Fire-in-the-hole!"* Three more explosions, even duller. Two grenades to each tunnel.

"Nobody's gonna be searching them buggers now."

The men laughed.

"Wouldn't find nothing anyway. A bag of rice, maybe some ammo. That's all."

"And maybe a goddamn mine, right?"

"Not worth it. Not worth my ass, damn sure."

"Well, no worry now. No way anybody's going down into *those* mothers."

"Ex-tunnels."

Another explosion, fifty yards away.

Then a succession of explosions, tearing apart huts; then yellow flashes, then white spears. Automatic rifle fire, short and incredibly close.

"See?" Barney said. He was lying beside me. "We did find 'em. We *did*."

"Surprised them," I said. "Faked 'em right out of their shoes."

"Incoming!"

Men were scrambling. Slow motion, then fast motion, and the whole village seemed to shake.

"Incoming!" It was Barney. He was peering at me, grinning. "Incoming!"

"Nice hollering."

On the perimeter of the village, the company began returning fire, blindly, spraying the hedges with M-16 and M-70 and M-60 fire. No targets, nothing to aim

16

at and kill. Aimlessly, just shooting to shoot. It had been going like this for weeks—snipers, quick little attacks, blind counterfire. Days, days. Those were the days.

"Cease fire," the lieutenants hollered.

"Cease fire," the platoon sergeants hollered.

"Cease the fuckin' fire," shouted the squad leaders.

"That," I told Barney, "is the chain of command."

And Barney smiled. His face had the smooth complexion of a baby brother. Tickle him and he'd coo.

When it ended, he and I walked over to where the mortar rounds had come in. Soldiers from the third platoon were standing there in the wreckage of huts and torn-down trees. It was over. Things happened, things came to an end. There was no sense of developing drama. All that remained was debris, four smouldering holes in the dirt, a few fires that would burn themselves out. "Nobody hurt," one of the men said. "Lucky thing. We was all sitting down—a little rest break, you know? Smokin' and snoozin'. Lucky, lucky thing. *Lucky*. Anybody standing up when that shit hits is dead. I mean gone." The soldier sat on his pack and opened a can of peaches. It was over. There was no fear left in him, or in any of us.

When the captain ran over to check on casualties, the same soldier repeated his story, making sure the captain understood the value of a good long rest break. Johansen smiled. What else was there to do? Smile, make a joke of it all. Blunder on. Captain Johansen told me to call battalion headquarters. "Just inform them that we're heading off for our night position. Don't mention this little firefight, okay? I don't want to waste time messing with gunships or artillery—what's the use?"

17

I made the call. Then we hefted our packs and guns, formed up into a loose column, and straggled out of the village.

It was only a two-hundred-meter march to the little wooded hill where we made our night position, but by the time the foxholes were dug and we'd eaten cold C rations, it had been dark for nearly an hour.

The day ended.

Now night came. Old rituals, old fears. Spooks and goblins. Sometimes at night there was the awful certainty that men would die at their foxholes or in their sleep, silently, not a peep, but this night everyone talked softly and bravely. No one doubted that we'd be hit, yet there was no real terror. We hadn't lost a man that day, even after eight hours of sniping and harassment, and the enemy's failure during the day made the dark hours easier. We simply waited. Taking turns at guard, careful not to light cigarettes, we waited until nearly daybreak. And then only a half-dozen mortar rounds came down. No casualties. We were charmed.

When it was light, a new day, Bates and Barney and I cooked C rations together. Same food, same smells. The heat was what woke us up. Then flies. Slowly, the camp came alive. The men stirred, lay on their backs, dreamed, talked in small groups. At that early hour no one kept guard: A glance out into the brush now and then, that was all. A cursory feign. It was like waking up in a cancer ward, no one ambitious to get on with the day, no one with obligations, no plans, nothing to hope for, no dreams for the daylight.

"Not a bad night, really," Barney said. "I mean, I was looking for the whole fuckin' Red Army to come thunking down on us. But zilch. A few measly mortar rounds."

Bates shrugged. "Maybe they're out of ammo."

"You think so?"

"Could be," Bates said. "A real possibility."

Barney stared at him, thinking, then he smiled. The idea excited him.

"You really think so?" he said. "Out *completely*?"

"No question about it." Bates put on a solemn face. He was a teaser and he loved going after Barney. "Way I figure it, pal, Uncle Charles shot his whole wad yesterday. Follow me? Boom, it's all gone. So today's *got* to be quiet. Simple logic."

"Yeah," Barney murmured. He kept wagging his head, stirring his ham and eggs. *"Yeah."*

"We wore 'em out. A war of fucking attrition."

Things were peaceful. There was only the sky and the heat and the coming day. Mornings were good.

We ate slowly. No reason to hurry, no reason to move. The day would be yesterday. Village would lead to village, and our feet would hurt, and we would do the things we did, and the day would end.

"Sleep okay?" Bates said.

"Until two hours ago. Something woke me up. Weird—sounded like somebody trying to kill me."

"Yeah," Barney said. "Sometimes I have bad dreams too."

And we gathered up our gear, doused the fires, saddled up, and found our places in the single file line of march. We left the hill and moved down into the first village of the day.

19

II

Pro Patria

I grew out of one war and into another. My father came from leaden ships of sea, from the Pacific theater; my mother was a WAVE. I was the offspring of the great campaign against the tyrants of the 1940's, one explosion in the Baby Boom, one of millions come to replace those who had just died. My bawling came with the first throaty note of a new army in spawning. I was bred with the haste and dispatch and careless muscle-flexing of a nation giving bridle to its own good fortune and success. I was fed by the spoils of 1945 victory.

I learned to read and write on the prairies of southern Minnesota.

Along the route used to settle South Dakota and the flatlands of Nebraska and northern Iowa, in the cold winters, I learned to use ice skates.

My teachers were brittle old ladies, classroom football coaches, flushed veterans of the war, pretty girls in sixth grade.

In patches of weed and clouds of imagination, I learned to play army games. Friends introduced me to the Army Surplus Store off main street. We bought dented relics of our fathers' history, rusted canteens and olive-scented, scarred helmet liners. Then we were our fathers, taking on the Japs and Krauts along the shores of Lake Okabena, on the flat fairways of the golf course. I rubbed my fingers across my father's war decorations, stole a tiny battle star off one of them and carried it in my pocket.

Baseball was for the summertime, when school ended. My father loved baseball. I was holding a Louisville Slugger when I was six. I played a desperate shortstop for the Rural Electric Association Little League team; my father coached us, and he is still coaching, still able to tick off the starting line-up of the great Brooklyn Dodgers teams of the 1950's.

Sparklers and the forbidden cherry bomb were for the Fourth of July: a baseball game, a picnic, a day in the city park, listening to the high school band playing "Anchors Aweigh," a speech, watching a parade of American Legionnaires. At night, fireworks erupted over the lake, reflections.

It had been Indian land. Ninety miles from Sioux City, sixty miles from Sioux Falls, eighty miles from Cherokee, forty miles from Spirit Lake and the site of a celebrated massacre. To the north was Pipestone and the annual Hiawatha Pageant. To the west was Luverne and Indian burial mounds.

Norwegians and Swedes and Germans had taken the plains from the Sioux. The settlers must have seen endless plains and eased their bones and said, "Here as well as anywhere, it's all the same."

The town became a place for wage earners. It is a place for wage earners today—not very spirited people, not very thoughtful people.

Among these people I learned about the Second World War, hearing it from men in front of the courthouse, from those who had fought it. The talk was tough. Nothing to do with causes or reason; the war was right, they muttered, and it had to be fought.

The talk was about bellies filled with German lead, about the long hike from Normandy to Berlin, about close calls and about the origins of scars just visible on hairy arms. Growing up, I learned about another war, a peninsular war in Korea, a gray war fought by the town's Lutherans and Baptists. I learned about that war when the town hero came home, riding in a convertible, sitting straight-backed and quiet, an ex-POW.

The town called itself Turkey Capital of the World. In September the governor and some congressmen came to town. People shut down their businesses and came in from their farms. Together we watched trombones and crepe-paper floats move down mainstreet. The bands and floats represented Sheldon, Tyler, Sibley, Jackson, and a dozen other neighboring towns.

Turkey Day climaxed when the farmers herded a billion strutting, stinking, beady-eyed birds down the center of town, past the old Gobbler Cafe, past Woolworth's and the Ben Franklin store and the Standard Oil service station. Feathers and droppings and popcorn mixed together in tribute to the town and the prairie. We were young. We stood on the curb and blasted the animals with ammunition from our peashooters.

We listened to Nelson Rockefeller and Karl Rölvaag and the commander of the Minnesota VFW, trying to make sense out of their words, then we went for twenty-five-cent rides on the Octopus and Tilt-A-Whirl.

I couldn't hit a baseball. Too small for football, but I stuck it out through junior high, hoping something would change. When nothing happened, I began to read. I read Plato and Erich Fromm, the Hardy boys and enough Aristotle to make me prefer Plato. The

town's library was quiet and not a very lively place—
nothing like the football field on an October evening
and not a very good substitute. I watched the athletes
from the stands and cheered them at pep rallies, wishing I were with them. I went to homecoming dances,
learned to drive an automobile, joined the debate
team, took girls to drive-in theaters and afterward to
the A & W root beer stand.

I took up an interest in politics. One evening I put
on a suit and drove down to the League of Women
Voters meeting, embarrassing myself and some candidates and most of the women voters by asking questions that had no answers.

I tried going to Democratic party meetings. I'd read
it was the liberal party. But it was futile. I could not
make out the difference between the people there and
the people down the street boosting Nixon and Cabot
Lodge. The essential thing about the prairie, I
learned, was that one part of it is like any other part.

At night I sometimes walked about the town. "God
is both transcendent and imminent. That's Tillich's
position." When I walked, I chose the darkest streets,
away from the street lights. "But is there a God? I
mean, is there a God like there's a tree or an apple?
Is God a being?" I usually ended up walking toward
the lake. "God is Being-Itself." The lake, Lake Okabena, reflected the town-itself, bouncing off a black-
and-white pattern identical to the whole desolate
prairie: flat, tepid, small, strangled by algae, shut in
by middle-class houses, lassoed by a ring of doctors,
lawyers, CPA's, dentists, drugstore owners, and pro-
prietors of department stores. "Being-Itself? Then is
this town God? It exists, doesn't it?" I walked past
where the pretty girls lived, stopping long enough to
look at their houses, all the lights off and the curtains

drawn. "Jesus," I muttered, "I hope not. Maybe I'm an atheist."

One day in May the high school held graduation ceremonies. Then I went away to college, and the town did not miss me much.

III

Beginning

The summer of 1968, the summer I turned into a soldier, was a good time for talking about war and peace. Eugene McCarthy was bringing quiet thought to the subject. He was winning votes in the primaries. College students were listening to him, and some of us tried to help out. Lyndon Johnson was almost forgotten, no longer forbidding or feared; Robert Kennedy was dead but not quite forgotten; Richard Nixon looked like a loser. With all the tragedy and change that summer, it was fine weather for discussion.

And, with all of this, there was an induction notice tucked into a corner of my billfold.

So with friends and acquaintances and townspeople, I spent the summer in Fred's antiseptic cafe, drinking coffee and mapping out arguments on Fred's napkins. Or I sat in Chic's tavern, drinking beer with kids from the farms. I played some golf and tore up the pool table down at the bowling alley, keeping an eye open for likely-looking high school girls.

Late at night, the town deserted, two or three of us would drive a car around and around the town's lake, talking about the war, very seriously, moving with care from one argument to the next, trying to make it a dialogue and not a debate. We covered all the big questions: justice, tyranny, self-determination, conscience and the state, God and war and love.

College friends came to visit: "Too bad, I hear you're drafted. What will you do?"

I said I didn't know, that I'd let time decide. Maybe something would change, maybe the war would end. Then we'd turn to discuss the matter, talking long, trying out the questions, sleeping late in the mornings.

The summer conversations, spiked with plenty of references to the philosophers and academicians of war, were thoughtful and long and complex and careful. But, in the end, careful and precise argumentation hurt me. It was painful to tread deliberately over all the axioms and assumptions and corollaries when the people on the town's draft board were calling me to duty, smiling so nicely.

"It won't be bad at all," they said. "Stop in and see us when it's over."

So to bring the conversations to a focus and also to try out in real words my secret fears, I argued for running away.

I was persuaded then, and I remain persuaded now, that the war was wrong. And since it was wrong and since people were dying as a result of it, it was evil. Doubts, of course, hedged all this: I had neither the expertise nor the wisdom to synthesize answers; the facts were clouded; there was no certainty as to the kind of government that would follow a North Vietnamese victory or, for that matter, an American victory, and the specifics of the conflict were hidden away—partly in men's minds, partly in the archives of government, and partly in buried, irretrievable history. The war, I thought, was wrongly conceived and poorly justified. But perhaps I was mistaken, and who really knew, anyway?

Piled on top of this was the town, my family, my teachers, a whole history of the prairie. Like magnets, these things pulled in one direction or the other, almost physical forces weighting the problem, so that, in the end, it was less reason and more gravity that was the final influence.

My family was careful that summer. The decision was mine and it was not talked about. The town lay there, spread out in the corn and watching me, the mouths of old women and Country Club men poised in readiness to find fault. It was not a town, not a Minneapolis or New York, where the son of a father can sometimes escape scrutiny. More, I owed the prairie something. For twenty-one years I'd lived under its laws, accepted its education, eaten its food, wasted and guzzled its water, slept well at night, driven across its highways, dirtied and breathed its air, wallowed in its luxuries. I'd played on its Little League teams. I remembered Plato's *Crito,* when Socrates, facing certain death—execution, not war—had the chance to escape. But he reminded himself that he had seventy years in which he could have left the country, if he were not satisfied or felt the agreements he'd made with it were unfair. He had not chosen Sparta or Crete. And, I reminded myself, I hadn't thought much about Canada until that summer.

The summer passed this way. Golden afternoons on the golf course, an illusive hopefulness that the war would grant me a last-minute reprieve, nights in the pool hall or drug store, talking with towns-folk, turning the questions over and over, being a philosopher.

Near the end of that summer the time came to go to the war. The family indulged in a cautious sort of Last Supper together, and afterward my father, who is brave, said it was time to report at the bus depot. I moped down to my bedroom and looked the place over, feeling quite stupid, thinking that my mother would come in there in a day or two and probably cry a little. I trudged back up to the kitchen and put my satchel down. Everyone gathered around, saying so long and good health and write and let us know if you want anything. My father took up the induction papers, checking on times and dates and all the last-minute things, and when I pecked my mother's face and grabbed the satchel for comfort, he told me to put it down, that I wasn't supposed to report until tomorrow. I'd misread the induction date.

After laughing about the mistake, after a flush of red color and a flood of ribbing and a wave of relief had come and gone, I took a long drive around the lake. Sunset Park, with its picnic table and little beach and a brown wood shelter and some families swimming. The Crippled Children's School. Slater Park, more kids. A long string of split level houses, painted every color.

The war and my person seemed like twins as I went around the town's lake. Twins grafted together and forever together, as if a separation would kill them both.

The thought made me angry.

In the basement of my house I found some scraps of cardboard. I printed obscene words on them. I declared my intention to have no part of Vietnam. With delightful viciousness, a secret will, I declared the war evil, the draft board evil, the town evil in its lethargic acceptance of it all. For many minutes, making up the signs, making up my mind, I was outside the town. I was outside the law. I imagined myself strutting up and down the sidewalks outside the

28

depot, the bus waiting and the driver blaring his horn, the *Daily Globe* photographer trying to push me into line with the other draftees, the frantic telephone calls, my head buzzing at the deed.

On the cardboard, my strokes of bright red were big and ferocious looking. The language was clear and certain and burned with a hard, defiant, criminal, blasphemous sound. I tried reading it aloud. I was scared. I was sad.

Later in the evening I tore the signs into pieces and put the shreds in the garbage can outside. I went back into the basement. I slipped the crayons into their box, the same stubs of color I'd used a long time before to chalk in reds and greens on Roy Rogers' cowboy boots.

I'd never been a demonstrator, except in the loose sense. True, I'd taken a stand in the school newspaper on the war, trying to show why it seemed wrong. But, mostly, I'd just listened.

"No war is worth losing your life for," a college acquaintance used to argue. "The issue isn't a moral one. It's a matter of efficiency: What's the most efficient way to stay alive when your nation is at war? That's the issue."

But others argued that no war is worth losing your country for, and when asked about the case when a country fights a wrong war, those people just shrugged.

Most of my college friends found easy paths away from the problem, all to their credit. Deferments for this and that. Letters from doctors or chaplains. It was hard to find people who had to think much about the problem. Counsel came from two main quarters, pacifists and veterans of foreign wars, but neither camp had much to offer. It wasn't a matter of peace, as the pacifists argued, but rather a matter of when and when not to join others in making war. And it wasn't a matter of listening to an ex-lieutenant colonel talk about serving in a right war, when the question was whether to serve in what seemed a wrong one.

On August 13, I went to the bus depot. A Worthington *Daily Globe* photographer took my picture standing by a rail fence with four other draftees.

Then the bus took us through corn fields, to little towns along the way—Rushmore and Adrian—where other recruits came aboard. With the tough guys drinking beer and howling in the back seats, brandishing their empty cans and calling one another "scum" and "trainee" and "GI Joe," with all this noise and hearty farewelling, we went to Sioux Falls. We spent the night in a YMCA. I went out alone for a beer, drank it in a corner booth, then I bought a book and read it in my room.

At noon the next day our hands were in the air, even the tough guys. We recited the oath—some of us loudly and daringly, others in bewilderment. It was a brightly lighted room, wood paneled. A flag gave the place the right colors. There was smoke in the air. We said the words, and we were soldiers.

I'd never been much of a fighter. I was afraid of bullies: frustrated anger. Still, I deferred to no one. Positively lorded myself over inferiors. And on top of that was the matter of conscience and conviction, uncertain and surface-deep but pure nonetheless. I was a confirmed liberal. Not a pacifist, but I would have cast my ballot to end the Vietnam war, I would have voted for Eugene McCarthy, hoping he would make peace. I was not soldier material, that was certain.

But I submitted. All the soul searchings and midnight conversations and books and beliefs were voided by abstention, extinguished by forfeiture, for lack of oxygen, by a sort of sleepwalking default. It was no decision, no chain of ideas or reasons, that steered me into the war.

It was an intellectual and physical stand-off, and I did not have the energy to see it to an end. I did not want to be a soldier, not even an observer to war. But neither did I want to upset a peculiar balance between the order I knew, the people I knew, and my own private world. It was not just that I valued that order. I also feared its opposite—inevitable chaos, censure, embarrassment, the end of everything that had happened in my life, the end of it all.

And the stand-off is still there. I would wish this book could take the form of a plea for everlasting peace, a plea from one who knows, from one who's been there and come back, an old soldier looking back at a dying war.

That would be good. It would be fine to integrate it all to persuade my younger brother and perhaps some others to say no to wrong wars.

Or it would be fine to confirm the old beliefs about war: It's horrible, but it's a crucible of men and events and, in the end, it makes more of a man out of you.

But, still, none of this seems right.

Now, war ended, all I am left with are simple, unprofound scraps of truth. Men die. Fear hurts and humiliates. It is hard to be brave. It is hard to know what bravery *is*. Dead human beings are heavy and awkward to carry, things smell different in Vietnam, soldiers are dreamers, drill sergeants are boors, some men thought the war was proper and others didn't and most didn't care. Is that the stuff for a morality lesson, even for a theme?

Do dreams offer lessons? Do nightmares have themes,

31

do we awaken and analyze them and live our lives and advise others as a result? Can the foot soldier teach anything important about war, merely for having been there? I think not. He can tell war stories.

IV

Nights

"Incoming," the lieutenant shouted.

We dove for a foxhole. I was first in, the earth taking care of my belly; the lieutenant and some others piled in on top of me.

Grenades burst around the perimeter, a few rifle shots.

"Wow, like a sandwich," I said. "Just stay where you are."

"Yep, we're nothing but sandbags for O'Brien," Mad Mark said, peering up to watch the explosions go off.

It didn't last long.

A blond-headed soldier ran over when the shooting ended. "Jesus, I got me a hunk of grenade shrapnel in my fuckin hand," he said. He sucked the wound. It didn't seem bad.

Mad Mark inspected the cut under a flashlight. "Will it kill you before morning?"

"Nope, I guess not. Have to get a tetanus shot, I suppose. Christ, those tetanus shots *hurt* don't they?"

As it turned out, the fire fight had not been a fire fight. The blond soldier and a few others had been bored. Bored all day. Bored that night. So they'd synchronized watches, set a time, agreed to toss hand grenades outside our perimeter at 2200 sharp, and when 2200 came, they did it, staging the battle. They shouted and squealed and fired their weapons and threw hand grenades and had a good time, making noise, scaring hell out of everyone. Something to talk about in the morning.

"Great little spat," they said the next day, slyly.

"Great?" I couldn't believe it.

"Ah, you know. Little action livens up everything, right? Gets the ol' blood boiling."

"You crazy?"

"Mad as a hatter."

"You like getting shot, for God's sake? You *like* Charlie trying to chuck grenades into your foxhole? You *like* that stuff?"

"Some got it, some don't. Me, I'm mad as a hatter."

"Don't let him shit you," Chip said. "That whole thing last night was a fake. They planned it, beginning to end."

"Except for old Turnip Head getting a piece of his own grenade," Bates said. "They didn't plan that." Bates walked along beside me, the platoon straggled out across a wide rice paddy. "Turnip Head threw his grenade and it hit a tree and bounced right back at him. Lucky he didn't blow his head off."

Chip shook his head. He was a short, skinny soldier from Orlando, Florida, a black guy. "Me, I don't take chances like that. You're right, they're nutty," he said.

We walked along. Forward with the left leg, plant the foot, lock the knee, arch the ankle. Push the leg into the paddy, stiffen the spine. Let the war rest there atop the left leg: the rucksack, the radio, the hand grenades, the magazines of golden ammo, the rifle, the steel helmet, the jingling dogtags, the body's own fat and water and meat, the whole contingent

34

of warring artifacts and flesh. Let it all perch there, rocking on top of the left leg, fastened and tied and anchored by latches and zippers and snaps and nylon cord.

Packhorse for the soul. The left leg does it all. Scolded and trained. The left leg stretches with magnificent energy, long muscle. Lumbers ahead. It's the strongest leg, the pivot. The right leg comes along, too, but only a companion. The right leg unfolds, swings out, and the right foot touches the ground for a moment, just quickly enough to keep pace with the left, then it weakens and raises on the soil a pattern of desolation.

Arms move about, taking up the rhythm.

Eyes sweep the rice paddy. Don't walk there, too soft. Not there, dangerous, mines. Step there and there and there, not there, step there and there and there, careful, careful, watch. Green ahead. Green lights, go. Eyes roll in the sockets. Protect the legs, no chances, watch for the fuckin snipers, watch for ambushes and punji pits. Eyes roll about, looking for mines and pieces of stray cloth and bombs and threads and things. Never blink the eyes, tape them open.

The stomach is on simmer, low flame. Fire down inside, down in the pit, just above the balls.

"Watch where you sit, now," the squad leader said. We stopped for shade. "Eat up quick, we're stopping for five minutes, no more."

"Five minutes? Where's the whips and chains?" Bates picked a piece of ground to sit on.

"Look," the squad leader sighed. "Don't get smart ass. I take orders, you know. Sooner we get to the night position, sooner we get resupplied, sooner we get to sleep, sooner we get this day over with. Sooner everything." The squad leader cleaned his face with a rag, rubbed his neck with it.

Barney joined us. "Why we stopping now?"

"Good," the squad leader said. "Someone here understands it's better to keep moving."

Bates laughed, an aristocrat. "I don't know about Buddy Barney, but actually, I was dreaming on the march. I was right in the middle of one. Daughter of this famous politician and me. Had her undressed on a beach down in the Bahamas. Jesus." He gestured vaguely, trying to make us see, sweeping away the heat with his hand. "Had her undressed, see? Her feet were just in the water, these luscious waves lapping up all around her toes and through the cracks between them, and she had this beach towel under her. The only thing she was wearing was sunglasses."

"You really think about politicians' daughters out here?" Barney asked.

"Lovely," Bates said. He closed his eyes.

We ate our noon C rations, then walked up a trail until the end of day.

We dug foxholes and laid our ponchos out.

Dark came. The mountains to the west dissolved— bright red, then pink, then gold, then gray, then gone—and Quang Ngai, the land, seemed to fold into itself. There were creases in the dusk: reflections, mysteries, ghosts. The land moved. Hedges and boulders and chunks of earth—they *moved*. Things shimmied and fluttered. Distortions? Or a special sort of insight, nighttime clarity? Grouped around our holes, we would focus on the dark. Squint, peer, concentrate. We would seek out shapes in the dark. Impose solidity. We would squeeze our eyes shut. What we could not see, we imagined. Then—only then—we would see the enemy. We would see Charlie in our heads: oiled up, ghostly, blending with the countryside, part of the land. We would listen. What was that sound coming from just beyond the range of vision? A hum? Chanting? We would blink and rub our eyes and wonder about the magic of this place. Levitation, rumblings in the night, shadows, hidden graves.

Now, with the dark solid, Bates and Barney and Chip and I kept the watch from a foxhole along the north perimeter.

The talk was hushed.

"Yeah," Barney was saying, "it's called a starlight scope. I been humping the mother for a week now. Must weigh a ton."

Barney pulled the scope from its black carrying case and handed it across to Chip.

"See there?" Barney said. "A *ton*, right?"

Chip held the machine, testing its weight. The scope was maybe two feet long, shaped like a blunt telescope, painted black. It looked like something out of science fiction.

"Damned if I know how it works," Barney said. "Fucking kaleidoscope or something."

"A stargazing gizmo," Chip said. He held the scope up to his eye. "Star light, star bright."

Bates laughed. "You got to take off the lens cap, man."

"Who needs it? I see fine. Real fine. First star I see tonight, wish I may—"

Bates grasped the scope, removed the lens cap, and began fiddling with the dials.

"Wish I may, wish I might," Chip chanted, "have the wish I wish tonight."

"Shit," Bates said.

The machine's insides were top secret, but the

principle seemed simple enough: Use the night's orphan light—stars, moonglow, reflections, faraway fires—to turn night into day. The scope contained a heavy battery that somehow juiced up the starlight, intensifying it, magically exposing the night's secrets.

Bates finished tinkering with the scope and handed it back to Chip.

"That better?"

"Wow."

"What's out there?"

"A peep show," Chip murmured. "Sweet, sweet stuff. Dancing soul sisters." He giggled and stared through the scope. "Star light, star bright."

"Don't *hog* it, man."

"Dreamland!"

"Come on, what do you *see*?"

"All the secrets. I see 'em all out there."

"Hey—"

"Fairy-tale land," Chip whispered. He was quiet for a time. He held the machine tight to his eye, scanning the night, clucking softly. "I *see*. Yeah, now I *see*."

"Evil."

"No, it's sweet, real nice." Chip giggled. "I see a circus. No shit, there's a circus out there. Charlie's all dressed up in clown suits. Oh, yeah, a real circus."

And we took turns using the starlight scope. First Bates, then Barney, then me. It was peculiar. The night was there for us to see. A strange, soft deadness. Nothing moved. That was one of the odd things—through the scope, nothing moved. The colors were green. Bright, translucent green like the instrument panel in a jet plane at night.

"It's not right," Bates murmured. "Seeing at night—there's something evil about it."

"Star light, star bright."

"And where's Charlie? Where's the fucking Grim Reaper?"

"First star I see tonight. Wish I may, wish I might, have the wish I wish tonight."

Chip went off to sleep. Soon Barney joined him, and together Bates and I used the scope.

I watched the green dancing night.

"I wish for peace," Bates said.

A green fire. The countryside burned green at night, and I saw it. I saw the clouds move. I saw the vast, deep sleep of the paddies. I saw how the land was just the land.

I laughed, and Bates laughed, and soon the lieutenant came over and told us to quiet down.

We put the scope back in its case.

"Who needs it?" Bates said.

For a time we just sat there. We watched the dark grow on itself, and we let our imaginations do the rest.

Then I crawled into my poncho, lay back, and said good night.

Bates cradled his rifle. He peered out at the dark.

"Night," he said.

V

Under the Mountain

To understand what happens among the mine fields of My Lai, you must know something about what happens in America. You must understand Fort Lewis, Washington. You must understand a thing called basic training. A college graduate in May of 1968, I was at Fort Lewis in mid-August. One hundred of us came. We watched one another's hair fall, we learned the word "sir," we learned to react to "To duh rear, HARCH!" Above us the sixty-mile-distant mountain stood to the sky, white and cold. The mountain was Rainier; it stood for freedom.

I made a friend, Erik, and together he and I stumbled through the first months of army life.

I was not looking for friendship at Fort Lewis. The people were boors. Trainees and drill sergeants and officers, no difference in kind. In that jungle of robots there could be no hope of finding friendship; no one could understand the brutality of the place. I did not want a friend, that was how it stood in the end. If the savages had captured me, they would not drag me into compatibility with their kind. Laughing and talking of hometowns and drag races and twin-cammed racing engines—all this was for the others. I did not like them, and there was no reason to like them. For the other trainees, it came too easy. They did more than adjust well; they thrived on basic training, thinking they were becoming men, joking at the bullyism, getting the drill sergeants to joke along with them. I held my own, not a whisper more. I hated the trainees even more than the captors. But I hated them *all*. Passionate, sad, desperate hate. I learned to march, but I learned alone. I gaped at the neat package of stupidity and arrogance at Fort Lewis. I was superior. I made no apologies for believing it. Without sympathy or compassion, I instructed my intellect and eyes: ignore the horde. I kept vigil against intrusion into my private life. I shunned the herd.

I mouthed the words, shaping my lips and tongue just so, perfect deception. But no noise came out. The failure to bellow "Yes, Drill Sergeant!" was a fist in the bastard's face. A point for the soul. Standing in formation after chow, I learned to smoke. It was a private pleasure. I concentrated on my lungs and taste buds and hands and thoughts.

I maintained silence.

I thought about a girl. After thinking, she became a woman, only months too late. I spent time comparing her hair to the color of sand just at dusk. That sort of thing. I counted the number of soldiers I would trade for her. I memorized. I memorized details of her smell. I memorized her letters, whole letters. Memorizing was a way to remember and a way to forget, a way to remain a stranger, only a visitor at Fort Lewis. I memorized a poem she sent me. It was a poem by Auden, and marching for shots and haircuts and clothing issue, I recited the poem, forging Auden's words with thoughts I pretended to be hers. I lied about her, pretending that she wrote the poem herself, for me. I compared her to characters out of books by Hemingway and Maugham. In her letters she claimed I created her out of the mind. The mind, she said, can make wonderful changes in the real stuff. So I hid from the drill sergeants, turned my back on the barracks, and wrote back to her.

I thought a little about Canada. I thought about refusing to carry a rifle.

I grew tired of independence.

One evening I asked Erik what he was reading. His shoes were shined, and he had his footlocker straight, and with half an hour before lights out, he was on his back looking at a book. Erik. Skinny, a deep voice, dressed in olive drab, calm. He said it was *The Mint*. "T. E. Lawrence. You know—Lawrence of Arabia. He went through crap like this. Basic training. It's a sort of how-to-do-it book." He said he was just paging through it, that he'd read the whole thing before, and he gave it to me. With *The Mint* I became a soldier, knew I was a soldier. I succumbed. Without a backward glance at privacy, I gave in to soldiering. I took on a friend, betraying in a sense my wonderful suffering.

Erik talked about poetry and philosophy and travel. But he talked about soldiering, too. We formed a coalition. It was mostly a coalition against the army, but we aimed also at the other trainees. The idea, loosely, was to preserve ourselves. It was a two-man war of survival, and we fought like guerrillas, jabbing in the lance, drawing a trickle of army blood, running like rabbits. We hid in the masses. Right under their bloodshot eyes. We exposed them, even if they were blind and deaf to it. We'd let them die of anemia, a little blood at a time. It was a war of resistance; the objective was to save our souls. Sometimes it meant hiding the remnants of conscience and consciousness behind battle cries, pretended servility, bare, clench-fisted obedience. Our private conversations were the cornerstone of the resistance, perhaps because talking about basic training in careful, honest words was by itself an insult to army education. Simply to think and talk and try to understand was evidence that we were not cattle or machines.

Erik pretended sometimes that he lacked the fundamental courage of the men of poetry and philosophy whom he read during the first nights at Fort Lewis.

"I was in Denmark when they drafted me. I did not want to come back. I wanted to become a European and write some books. There was even a chance for romance over there. But I come from a small town, my parents know everyone, and I couldn't hurt and embarrass them. And, of course, I was afraid."

Perhaps it was fear and perhaps it was good sense. Anyway, Erik and I rarely brought our war into the offensive stage, and when we were so stupid as to try, we were massacred like mice. One morning Erik cornered the company drill sergeant, a man named Blyton, and demanded an appointment, a private talk. Blyton hustled Erik through a door.

Erik informed him of his opposition to the Vietnam war. Erik explained that he believed the war was without just reason, that life ought not to be forfeited unless certain and fundamental principles are at stake, and not unless those principles stand in certain danger.

Erik did not talk to me about the episode for a week or more. And when he did talk, he only said that Blyton laughed at him and then yelled and called him a coward.

"He said I was a pansy. It's hard to argue, I suppose. I'm not just intellectually opposed to violence,

I'm absolutely frightened by it. It's impossible to separate in my mind the gut fear from pure reason. I'm really afraid that all the hard, sober arguments I have against this war are nothing but an intellectual adjustment to my horror at the thought of bleeding to death in some rice paddy."

Blyton did not forget Erik, and we had to take the guerrilla war to the mountain for a while. We were good boys, good soldiers. We assumed a tranquil mediocrity. We returned to our detached, personal struggle.

We found a private place to talk, out behind the barracks. There was a log there. It was twice the thickness of an ordinary telephone pole and perhaps a fourth its length, and on an afternoon in September Erik and I were sitting on that log, polishing boots, cleaning our M-14s and talking poetry. It was a fine log, and useful. We used it for a podium and as a soapbox. It was a confessional and a shoeshine stand. It was scarred. A hundred waves of men had passed through the training company before us; no reason to doubt that a hundred waves would follow.

On that September afternoon Erik smeared black polish onto the log, marking it with our presence, and absently he rubbed at the stain, talking about poems. He explained (and he'll forgive my imprecise memory as I quote him now): "Frost, by just about any standard, is the finest of a good bunch of American poets. People who deprecate American poetry need to return to Robert Frost. Then, as I rank them —let's see—Marianne Moore and Robinson. And if you count Pound as an American, he has written the truest of poems. For all his mistakes, despite his wartime words on the radio, that man sees through ideology like you and I look through glass. If you don't believe, just listen."

Erik became Ezra Pound. Seriously, slowly, he recited a portion of "Hugh Selwyn Mauberly"

> These fought in any case,
> and some believing,
>   pro domo, in any case . . .
>
> Some quick to arm,
> some for adventure,
> some from fear of weakness,
> some from fear of censure,
> some for love of slaughter, in imagination,
> learning later . . .
> some in fear, learning love of slaughter;
>
> Died some, pro patria,
>   non "dulce" non "et decor" . . .

"Pound is right," Erik said. "Look into your own history. Here we are. Mama has been kissed good-bye, we've grabbed our rifles, we're ready for war. All this not because of conviction, not for ideology; rather it's from fear of society's censure, just as Pound claims. Fear of weakness. Fear that to avoid war is to avoid manhood. We come to Fort Lewis afraid to admit we are not Achilles, that we are not brave, not heroes. Here we are, thrust to the opposite and absurd antipode of what we think is good. And tomorrow we'll be out of bed at three o'clock in the pitch-black morning."

"Up, up, up!" the squad leader shouts. He has been in the army for two weeks, same as the rest of us. But he is big and he is strong and he is in charge. He loves the new power. "Out of the sack! Out!"

"Ya damn lifer!" It is Harry the Montanan, head under a sheet, pointing a thick middle finger at the squad leader's back. "Lifer! Ya hear me? Take yer damn army an' shove it. Use it fer grade-Z fertilizer!" Harry pauses. The squad leader hits the lights, glaring and cold and excruciatingly bright lights. Harry shoves his face into the pillow. "Two-bit goddamn lifer!"

The squad leader orders Harry to scrub the commodes. Harry threatens to use the squad leader's head as a scrub brush.

The squad leader is chastened but still in charge. "Okay, who's gonna wax the floor?" He checks his duty roster, finds a name.

Mousy whines. "Well, for Pete's sake, they got the buffer downstairs. What the hell you want? Want me to polish the damn thing with a sock?"

"Use yer brown nose," the Montanan drawls, head still tucked into a pillow.

White paddles over to the shower. You hear him singing about Idaho. He was married two days before induction.

Mornings are the worst time. It is the most hopeless, most despairing time. The darkness of Fort Lewis mornings is choked off by brazen lights, the shrieks of angry men and frightened, homesick boys. The bones and muscles and brain are not ready for three-o'clock mornings, not ready for duties and harsh voices. The petty urgencies of the mornings physically hurt. The same hopeless feeling that must have overwhelmed inmates of Treblinka: unwilling to escape and yet unwilling to acquiesce, no one to help, no consolation. The reality of the morning kills words.

46

In the mornings at Fort Lewis comes a powerful want for privacy. You pledge yourself to finding an island someday. Or a bolted, sealed, air-conditioned hotel room. No lights, no admittance, no friends, not even your girl, and not even Erik or your starving grandmother.

The men search out cheer. The North Dakotan bellows out that we may be going to the PX that night.

"Yeah, maybe!" Harry rolls onto the floor. "Second Platoon went last night. That makes it our turn, damn right. Christ, I'll buy me a million wads o' chewin' tobacco. An' a case o' Coke. Y'all gotta help me smuggle the stuff in here, right? Hide it in the footlockers."

We make up the bunks. Taut, creases at a forty-five-degree angle. Tempers flare, ebb into despair.

"KLINE!" someone hollers. "Kline, you're a goddamn moron! A goddamn, blubbering moron. You know that? Kline, you hear me? You're a moron!"

Kline stands by his bunk. His tiny head goes rigid. His hands fidget. His eyes shift to the floor, to the walls, to a footlocker. He whimpers. He quivers. Kline is fat. Bewildered and timid and sensitive. No one knows.

"Kline, you got two left boots on your feet. You see that? Look down, just look down once, will ya? You see your feet? You got two left boots on again. You see? Look down, for Christ's sake! Stop starin' around like you got caught snitchin' the lieutenant's pussy. There, ya see? Two left boots."

Kline grins and sits on his bunk. The problem isn't serious.

We make the bunks, dust the windows, tie up laundry bags, the strings anchored just so. The barracks have a high ceiling, crisscrossed by rafters and two-by-fours with no function except to give work. They have to be cleaned. The seventeen-year olds, most agile and awed, do the climbing and balancing. The squad leader directs them: a peer and a sellout. Sweep and mop and wax the floor. Polish doorknobs, rub the army's Brasso into metal.

The squad leader glances at his watch, frenzied. "Jeez, you guys, it's four-thirty already. Let's go, damn it."

We align footgear into neat rows, shave, polish our brass, buff-buff-buff that floor.

Outside it is Monday morning, raining again. Fort Lewis.

It is dark, and we are shadows double-timing to the parade ground for reveille. Someone pushes Kline into place at the end of a rank. "Good God, it's freezin'." Kline practices coming to attention. Christ, he tries.

We shiver, stamping blood into our feet. Erik stands next to me. He is quiet, smoking, calm, ready.

Smells twist through the rain. Someone in the back rank cusses; forgot to lock his footlocker. KP is the penalty. Someone asks for a smoke.

"Fall in! Re-port!"

Afterward Drill Sergeant Blyton struts his sleek, black, airborne body up and down the ranks. We hate Blyton. It is dark and it is gushing rain, and with our heads rammed straight ahead, Blyton is only a smudge of a Smokey-the-Bear hat, a set of gleaming teeth. He teases, threatens, humiliates. It is supposed to be an inspection. But it is much more than that, nearly life and death, and Blyton is the judge. It is supposed to be a part of the training. Discipline. Blyton is supposed to play a role, to make himself hated. But for Blyton it is much more. He is evil. He does not personify the tough drill sergeant; rather he is the army; he's the devil. Erik mutters that we'll get the bastard someday. Words will kill him.

Blyton finds Kline. The poor boy, towering above the drill sergeant and shifting his eyes to the left and right, up and down, whimpers. Kline is terrified. He shifts from one foot to the other. Blyton peers at him, at his belt buckle, at his feet. At his two left boots.

Blyton has Kline hang on to his left foot for an hour.

During the days and during the nights, we march. And sing. There are a thousand songs.

> Around her hair
> She wore a yellow bonnet.
> She wore it in the springtime,
> In the merry month of May.
> And if
> You ask
> Her
> Why the hell she wore it:
> She wore it for her soldier
> Who was far, far away.

You write beautifully, a girl says in her letters. You make it all so terrible and real for me. . . . I am going to Europe next summer, she writes, and I'll see a lot of places for you. As ever . . .

> If I had a low IQ,
> I could be a Lifer, too!
> And if I didn't have a brain,
> I would learn to love the rain.

Am I right or wrong?
Am I goin' strong?
Sound off!
Sound off!
One, two, three, four . . .
Sound Off!

We march to the night infiltration course. They use machine guns on us, firing overhead while Erik and Harry and White and Kline crawl alongside me, under barbed wire, red tracers everywhere, down into ditches, across the finish line. In the rain. Then in dead night we march back to the barracks.

Viet-nam
Viet-nam
Every night while you're sleepin'
Charlie Cong comes a-creepin'
All around.

We march to the Quick-Kill rifle range. We learn to snap off our shots, quickly, rapidly, without aim. Without any thought at all. Quick-Kill.

We march to the obstacle course, and Blyton shoves Kline through the maneuvers.

We march back to the barracks, and we are always singing.

If I die in a combat zone,
Box me up and ship me home.
An' if I die on the Russian front,
Bury me with a Russian cunt.

Sound Off!

We march to the bayonet course, through green forests, through the ever-rain and through smells of loam and leaves and pine and every fine scent of nature, marching like wind-up toys under the free, white mountain, Rainier.

Blyton teaches us and taunts us. Standing with his legs spread wide on an elevated platform, he gives us our lesson in the bayonet. Left elbow locked, left hand on wood just below weapon's sights, right hand on small of stock, right forearm pressed tightly along the upper stock, lunge with left leg, slice up with the steel. Again and again we thrust into mid-air imagined bellies, sometimes toward throats. "Dinks are little shits," Blyton yells out. "If you want their guts, you gotta go low. Crouch and dig."

"Soldiers! Tell me! What is the spirit of the bayonet?" He screams the question, rolling it like Sandburg's poetry, thundering.

Raise your rifle, blade affixed, raise it high over your head, wave it like a flag or trophy, wave it in love, and bellow till you're hoarse: "Drill Sergeant, the spirit of the bayonet is to kill! To kill!"

> I know a girl, name is Jill,
> She won't do it, but her sister will.
> Honey, oh, Baby-Doll.
>
> I know a girl, dressed in black,
> Makes her living on her back.
> Honey, oh, Baby-Doll.
>
> I know a girl, dressed in red,
> Makes her living in a bed.
> Honey, oh, Baby-Doll.

51

There is no thing named love in the world. Women are dinks. Women are villains. They are creatures akin to Communists and yellow-skinned people and hippies. We march off to learn about hand-to-hand combat. Blyton grins and teases and hollers out his nursery rhyme: "If ya wanta live, ya gotta be ag-ile, mo-bile, and hos-tile." We chant the words: ag-ile, mo-bile, hos-tile. We make it all rhyme. We march away, singing.

> I don't know, but I been told,
> Eskimo pussy is mighty cold.
> Am I goin' strong?
> Am I right or wrong?
> Sound Off!

The company forms up for inspection. The battalion commander comes by in his dark glasses, and Blyton and the others are firm and mellow. We've been given instructions to say "No, sir" when the colonel asks if we have any problems or any complaints or any needs. When he asks if there's enough food and if we get enough sleep, we're supposed to say "Yes, sir."

They stuff us into the barracks at ten o'clock. The squad leader gears us up for nighttime cleaning. He promises to allow an extra half-hour of sleep in the morning, and we know he's lying, but the floor gets waxed and our shoes get shined and the lockers get wiped.

Blyton comes in and cusses and turns the light off and by eleven o'clock all the boors and bullies snort their way to sleep. It is a cattle pen. A giant rhythm takes up the barracks, a swelling and murmuring of hearts and lungs; the wooden planks seem to move, in and out. You fight to hold to the minutes. Sleep is an enemy. Sleep puts you with the rest of them, the great, public, hopeless zoo. You battle the body. Then you sleep.

But in the heart of sleep, you are awakened.

Fire watch.

You sit on the darkened stairs between the two tiers of bunks, and you smoke. Fire watch is good duty. You lose sleep, but the silence and letter-writing time and privacy make up for it, and you are free for an hour.

The rain is falling; you feel comfortable. You listen, smiling and smoking. Will you go to war? You think of Socrates; you see him beside you, stepping through basic training as your friend. He would be a joke in short hair and fatigues. He would not succumb. He would march through the days and nights in his white robes, with a white beard, and certainly Blyton would never break him. Socrates had fought for Athens: It could not have been a perfectly just war, but Socrates, it has been told, was a brave soldier. You wonder if he had been a reluctant hero. Had he been brave out of a spirit of righteousness? Or necessity? Or resignation? You wonder how he felt as a soldier on a night like this one, with the rain falling, with just this temperature and sound. Then you think of him as an old man, you remember his fate, you think of him peering through iron bars as his ship sailed in, the final cue, only extinction ahead; his country, for which he had been a hero, ending the most certain of good lives. Nothing recorded about his weeping. But Plato may have missed something. Certainly, he must have missed something. You think about other heroes. John Kennedy, Audie Murphy, Sergeant York, T. E. Lawrence. You write letters to blond girls from middle America, calm and poetic and filled with ironies and self-pity, then you smoke, then you rouse out Kline for the next watch.

Erik and I were discussing these things on that September afternoon, sitting behind the barracks and separating ourselves from everyone and putting polish on our boots, when Blyton saw us alone. He screamed and told us to get our asses over to him pronto.

"A couple of college pussies," he said when we got there. "Out behind them barracks hiding from everyone and making some love, huh?" He looked at Erik. "You're a pussy, huh? You afraid to be in the war, a goddamn pussy, a goddamn lezzie? You know what we do with pussies, huh? We fuck 'em. In the army we just fuck 'em and straighten 'em out. You two college pussies out there hidin' and sneakin' a little pussy. Maybe I'll just stick you two puss in the same bunk tonight, let you get plenty of pussy so tomorrow you can't piss." Blyton grinned and shook his head and said "shit" and called another drill sergeant over and told him he had a couple of pussies and wanted to know what to do. "They was out there behind the barracks suckin' in some pussy. What the hell we do with puss in the army? We fuck 'em, don't we? Huh? College puss almost ain't good enough for good fuckin'."

Erik said we were just polishing boots and cleaning our guns, and Blyton grabbed a rifle, stopped grinning, and had us chant, pointing at the rifle and at our bodies, "This is a rifle and this is a gun, this is for shooting and this is for fun." Then he told us to report to him that night. "You two puss are gonna have a helluva time. You're gonna get to pull guard together, all alone and in the dark, nobody watchin'. You two are gonna walk 'round and 'round the company area, holdin' hands, and you can talk about politics and nooky all the goddamn night. Shit, I wish I had a goddamn camera."

We reported to Blyton at 2100 hours, and he gave us a flashlight and black guard helmets and told us to get the hell out of his sight, he couldn't stand to look at pussy.

Outside, we laughed. Erik said the bastard didn't have the guts to order us to hold hands.

We put on the black helmets, snapped on the flashlight, and began making the rounds of the company area. It was a good, dry night. Things were peaceful. For more than two hours, we walked and enjoyed the night. No barracks quarrels, no noise. A sense of privacy and peace. We talked about whatever came to mind—our families, the coming war, hopes for the future, books, people, girls—and it was a good time. We felt . . . what? Free. In control. Pardoned. We walked and walked, not talking when there was no desire to talk, talking when the words came, walking, pretending it was the deep woods, a midnight hike, just walking and feeling good.

Much later, after perhaps fifty turns around the company area, we stumbled across a trainee making an unauthorized phone call. We debated about whether to turn the poor kid in. On the one hand, we sympathized; on the other hand, we were tired and it was late and our feet were hurting and we had a hunch that the kid's punishment would be to relieve us for the night. We gave Blyton the man's name. In twenty minutes the kid came out, asked for the flashlight, and told us to go to bed. We laughed.

We congratulated ourselves. We felt smart. And later —much later—we wondered if maybe Blyton hadn't won a big victory that night.

Basic training nearly ended, we marched finally to a processing station. We heard our numbers called off, our new names. Some to go to transportation school—Erik. Some to repeat basic training—Kline. Some to become mechanics. Some to become clerks. And some to attend advanced infantry training, to become foot soldiers—Harry and the squad leader and I. Then we marched to graduation ceremonies, and then we marched back, singing.

> I wanna go to Vietnam
> Just to kill ol' Charlie Cong.
> Am I right or wrong?
> Am I goin' strong?

Buses—olive drab, with white painted numbers and driven by bored-looking Spec 4's—came to take us away. Erik and I stood by a window in the barracks and watched Blyton talk with parents of the new soldiers. He was smiling.

"We'll get the bastard," Erik said. We could've picked off the man with one shot from an M-14, no problem. He'd taught us well. We laughed and shook our fists at the window. Too easy to shoot him.

"There's not much I can say to you," Erik said. "I had this awful suspicion they'd screw you, make you a grunt. Maybe you can break a leg during advanced training; pretend you're insane." Erik had decided at the beginning of basic to enlist for an extra year so as to escape infantry duty. I had gambled, thinking they would use me for more than a pair of legs, certain that someone would see the value of my ass behind a typewriter or a Xerox machine. We'd joked about the gamble for two months.

He had won, I had lost.

I shook Erik's hand in the latrine and walked with him to his bus and shook his hand again.

VI

Escape

In advanced infantry training, the soldier learns new ways to kill.

Claymore mines, booby traps, the M-60 machine gun, the M-70 grenade launcher, the .45-caliber pistol, the M-16 automatic rifle.

On the outside, AIT looks like basic training. Lots of push-ups, lots of shoe-shining and firing ranges and midnight marches. But AIT is not basic training. The difference is the certainty of going to war: pending doom that comes in with each day's light and lingers all the day long.

The soldier who finds himself in AIT is a marked man, and he knows it and thinks about it. War, a real war. The drill sergeant said it when we formed up for our first inspection: Every swinging dick in the company was now a foot soldier, a grunt in the United States Army, the infantry, Queen of Battle. Not a cook in the lot, not a clerk or mechanic among us. And in eight weeks, he said, we were all getting on a plane bound for Nam.

"I don't want you to mope around thinkin' about Germany or London," he told us. "Don't even *think* about it, 'cause there just ain't no way. You're leg men now, and we don't need no infantry in Piccadilly or Southampton. Besides, Vietnam ain't all that bad. I been over there twice now, and I'm alive and still screwin' everything in sight. You troops pay attention to the trainin' you get here, and you'll come back in one piece, believe me. Just pay attention, try to learn something. The Nam, it ain't so bad, not if you got your shit together."

One of the trainees asked him about rumors that we'd be shipped to Frankfort.

"Christ, you'll hear that crap till it makes you puke. Forget it. You dudes are Nam-bound. Warsville, understand? Death City. Every last fat swingin' dick."

Someone raised a hand and asked when we'd get our first pass.

"Get your gear into the barracks, sweep the place down, and you'll be out of here in an hour."

I went to the library in Tacoma. I found the *Reader's Guide* and looked up the section on the United States Army. Under the heading "AWOL and Desertion" I found the stuff I was looking for.

The librarian fetched out old copies of *Newsweek* and *Time,* and I went into a corner and made notes.

Most of the articles were nothing more than interviews with deserters, stories of their lives in Stockholm, where they lived openly, or in Paris, where they hid and used assumed names and grew beards. That was interesting reading—I was concerned with their psychology and with what compelled them to pack up and leave—but I needed something more concrete. I was after details, how-to-do-it stuff. I wanted to know the laws of the various nations, which countries would take deserters, and under what conditions. In one of the *Time* pieces I found a list of certain organizations in Sweden and Denmark and Holland that had been set up to give aid to American deserters. I wrote down the names and addresses.

Another article outlined the best routes into Canada, places where deserting GI's crossed. None of the NATO nations would accept U.S. military deserters; some sort of a mutual extradition pact was in force. I knew Canada harbored draft dodgers, but I couldn't find anything on their policy toward deserters, and I doubted our northern neighbors went that far. Sweden, despite all the problems of adjustment and employment, seemed the best bet.

I smiled at the librarian when I returned the magazines; then I went into the library's lobby and called the bus depot. To be sure, I disguised my voice—perhaps they had some sort of tape-recording system—and asked about rates and time schedules for Vancouver. From Seattle, Vancouver was only a two-hour drive, the fellow said, and the rates were low and buses ran frequently, even during the night.

Then I called the Seattle airport and checked on fares to Dublin, Ireland. Playing it carefully, professionally, I inquired first with one of the large American firms, telling them I was a student and wanted to do research overseas. Then I called Air Canada, gave them the same story, and mentioned that I might want to leave from Vancouver. Soon I had a list of airfares to more than a half-dozen European cities.

Having done all this, I went back to my corner in the library and, for the first time, persuaded myself that it was truly possible. No one would stop me at the Canadian border, not in a bus. A flight to Ireland would raise no suspicions. From Ireland it was only a day or two by boat to Sweden. There was no doubt it could be done.

I wrote a letter to my parents, and in the middle of it I asked them to send my passport and immunization card. I'd been to Europe in the summer of 1967, back when travel was fun and not flight. I told them I needed the passport for R & R when I got to Vietnam. I said the shot card was necessary for my army health records.

I itemized the expenses. Five hundred dollars would pull it off. I was two hundred dollars short, but I could find a job in Vancouver and have the balance in two weeks. Or, if I didn't want to waste the time, there were college people and old friends to borrow from.

It was dark when I left the Tacoma library.

Fort Lewis in the winter is sloppy and dirty. It's wet and very cold, and those things together make your gloves freeze on the firing ranges. On bivouac your sleeping bag stiffens. It's no fun to smoke—too much trouble to get the pack out. Better to stand and wiggle your fingers. You ride around the base in open cattle trucks, everyone bunched together like the animals that are supposed to ride there, and you don't say anything, just watch the trees, big lush pines in the snow. You start muttering to yourself. You wish you had a friend. You feel alone and sad and scared and desperate. You want to run.

The days are the same. You wear a uniform, you march, you shoot a rifle, but you aren't a soldier. Not really. You don't *belong* here. Some ghastly mistake.

Just before Thanksgiving I received the passport and immunization card from my parents, and on the same day I asked to see the battalion commander.

61

The first sergeant arranged it, grudgingly—because some regulation said he had no choice. But he ordered me to see the chaplain first.

"The chaplain weeds out the pussies from men with real problems," he said. "Seems this last year we been using too much shit on the crop. It's all coming up pussies, and the poor chaplain over there in his little church is busy as hell, just trying to weed out all you pussies. Good Lord ought to take pity on the chaplain, ought to stop manufacturing so damn many pussies up there."

The chaplain was named Edwards. He had thick red hair, a firm handshake, a disciplined but friendly mouth and a plump belly. Edwards was a man designed to soothe trainees, custom-made.

"What's the problem, mess hall not dishing out the bennies?" Edwards was trying to soften me up, trying to make me like him, trying to turn the problem into something not really worth pressing, trying to make all problems buckle under the weight of a friendly, God-fearing, red-headed officer. How often does an officer joke with you, man-to-man?

Smiling and saying no sir, my real problem is one of conscience and philosophy and intellect and emotion and fear and physical hurt and a desire to live chastened by a desire to be good, and also, underneath, a desire to prove myself a hero, I explained, in the broadest terms, what troubled me. Edwards listened and nodded. He took notes, and smiled whenever I smiled, and with his encouragement I gained steam and made my case. Which was: Chaplain, I believe human life is very valuable. I believe, and this has no final truth to it, that human life is valuable because, unlike the other species, we know good from bad; because men are aware they should pursue the good and not the bad; and because, often, people do in fact try to pursue the good, even if the pursuit brings painful personal consequences. I believe, therefore, that a man is most a man when he tries to recognize and understand what is good—when he tries to ask in a reasonable way about things: Is it good? And I believe, finally, that a man cannot be fully a man until he *acts* in the pursuit of goodness.

Chaplain, I think the war is wrong. I should not fight in it.

Now, we can debate the reasons for my beliefs, of course, and I'll be willing to do that, but, remember, sir, time is short, very short now. I go to Nam in two months.

Anyway, I'd prefer not to talk about these beliefs, because, I'm sorry to say this, I don't think you'll change my mind. I mean, maybe you will, of course. And I can't turn down a discussion of the war, not if you want it, not if you think that's the only thing you can do. But I fear we'll find ourselves arguing. And I can't argue with an officer, even a chaplain, so I'd rather just avoid talking about the rationale itself.

Instead, consider what advice you can offer about action, good-doing. Specifically? Specifically, I'm here to ask you if you see any flaw in a philosophy which says: the way to Emerald City, the way to God, the way to kill the wicked witch is to obey our reasoned judgments. Is there an alternative?

"Faith," he said. He nodded gravely, and, standing up, he said it again: "Faith, that does it."

"Faith? That's all you've got to say?"

"Well," he said, "I'm a chaplain, but, like you say, I'm also an officer. A captain in the U.S. Army. And I think you're not only wrong but, frankly, I think you're very disturbed, very disturbed. Not mental, you understand—I don't mean that. See . . . you've read too many books, the wrong ones, I think there's no doubt, the wrong ones. But goddamn it—pardon me—but goddamn it, you're a soldier now, and you'll sure as hell act like one! Some faith, some discipline. You know, this country is a good country. It's built on armies, just like the Romans and the Greeks and every other country. They're all built on armies. Or navies. They do what the country says. That's where faith comes in, you see? If you accept, as I do, that America is one helluva great country, well, then, you follow what she tells you. She says fight, then you go out and do your damnedest. You try to win." Edwards smiled with each of the mild expletives, toning them down, showing that he wasn't too distant, that he was in contact with the real world, and no prissy preacher. "Do you follow? It's a simple principle. Faith. When you get down to it, faith is an ancient Christian principle. I think it originated with Christ himself. Anyway, it was certainly faith that moved the crusaders way back when. Faith kept them going, God knows. Anyone who's read Norah Lofts and Thomas Costain knows that. Or history. You've been to college. Don't they read about Peter the Hermit anymore? Well, Peter the Hermit raised an army, led the men himself, and they marched a thousand miles to win back the holy city. Hell, do you think he sat in his monastery and thought it all out? He believed."

"Is that an analogy?" I asked. "Is Vietnam another Christian crusade?"

Edwards was angry. "You think I'm a fascist? You must think something like that. These days all soldiers and ministers are fascists, anti-intellectuals." He pulled out a handkerchief and wiped his red forehead like a gas station attendant doing a windshield. "Of course Vietnam is no crusade for Christ. Maybe the hippies are right, maybe no war is really fought for God. But there's still faith, and you've got to have it. You've got to have faith in somebody. Sometime, O'Brien, you'll realize there's something above, far above your puny intellect. Even if you're another Einstein or Galileo."

"This war was conceived in man's intellect," I said. "Someone decided to fight. Lyndon Johnson or Bundy or Rostow or Rusk or McNamara or Taylor—one of those guys *decided*."

"What about McKinley? McKinley prayed. The Spanish-American War wasn't some cold-blooded human decision. President McKinley waited and waited. He prayed to the Lord, asking for guidance, and the Lord finally told him to go to war."

"We read different books."

"Different books hell! That's history."

"That is McKinley's history."

Captain Edwards shouted. "All right, Private O'Brien, goddamn it, who do you read? Who the hell tells you the war is wrong?"

Calling me "Private O'Brien" was a cue. "Sir, I read the newspapers. There's a presidential campaign on. Vietnam is the big issue, almost the only issue, and I listen to the speeches. I supported McCarthy for the presidency, so I heard him talk about the war. I've read books by Bernard Fall—"

"Bernard Fall," Edwards shouted. "I've read Bernard Fall. He's a *professor*. A lousy *teacher*. Look, what do you know about communism, O'Brien? Do you think they're a bunch of friendly, harmless politicians, all ready to be friends and buddies? I've been in Russia, I've seen how people live there, so I know a little about this thing. You think Ho Chi Minh is gonna bring *heaven* to South Vietnam?"

"Well, sir, there's little evidence that South Vietnam under the communists will be a worse place than a South Vietnam ruled by a Diem or a Khanh. I mean, there's no persuasive evidence, at least not persuasive to me, that all the lives being lost, the children napalmed and everything—there's no good evidence that all this horror is worth preventing a change from Thieu to Ho Chi Minh. You see? I look for the bulk of evidence. I see evil in the history of Ho's rule of the north. I see evil in the history of the string of rulers we've helped in the South. Evil on both sides. But the third evil, the death and pain, must also be counted in."

"O'Brien, I'm surprised to hear this, really. You seem like a nice fellow. But, listen, you're betraying your country when you say these things. I've met people who don't like Vietnam, sure, but you're icy about it. Where the hell do you fit guts and bravery into your scheme? Where does God and the unknown fit in? Listen, I've *been* in Vietnam. I can tell you, this is a fine, heroic moment for American soldiers."

"Sir, if we could just forget the details. All I want is some advice. I don't think we can convince each other of anything, not about politics. But assuming, sir—just assuming—that I truly believe the war is wrong. Is it then also wrong to go off and kill people? If I do that, what happens to my soul? And if I don't fight, if I refuse, then I've betrayed my country, right?"

Captain Edwards glared at me. He slammed his fist on the desk. He picked up his telephone, still glaring. With cold civility he called battalion headquarters and made an appointment for me with the big man.

A staff car from headquarters came to get me. It pulled up in front of the chapel. A buck sergeant opened the back door and stood respectfully while the chaplain walked me down the steps, apologizing for getting angry. "Things are tough just now," he said. "There aren't enough chaplains to go around anymore. Really, we need a chaplain for every platoon. I guess the men are taking war more seriously than they used to—the young kids, the recruits. They need people, people with a little authority to get things done. Leaves and passes and things. But there's so damn many kids who want help, I get tired." He shook my hand, I saluted. "Listen, O'Brien, I like your style. I'm sincere about that, you've got a good story. You've got my respect, and you can expect me to follow you for the next few months. Stop in when you get back from Vietnam, we can talk some more then."

"You know, the Korean war and the Vietnam war aren't much different. One country divided by an artificial line. People of the same race killing each other. Communist aid, American aid. Communist troops, American troops. In both places the Reds got greedy. Oh sure, Vietnam is a whole new brand of fighting, guerrilla warfare, but we're learning it, we're getting good at it. I've served Uncle Sam in Korea and I've served him in Vietnam, three times. Let me tell you, Private, the wars are the same. The Chinese are behind these Asian wars. Private, you have dandruff on your uniform, brush it off. It's good we're stopping the Chinese when we have the chance. If it's not in South Vietnam, well, like the Aussie officers tell me, it'll be on the streets of Sydney."

The battalion commander chuckled. He wore dark

green sunglasses, and his eyes may have been closed. "The Chinese don't know much about street fighting, though. Hell, we'd kill them. We learned all that in Europe. Shit, you should have seen St. Vith, that was street fighting. Here, let me get that dandruff, it's all over your collar . . . there, now you're a strack trooper, just button up your pocket."

On the wall behind him a long train of photographs peered out, the chain of command. It started with Lyndon Johnson. Earl Wheeler, Stanley Reser, the Sixth Army commander, the fort commander, and finally the razor-lipped, hint-of-a-smile face of the battalion commander.

"But you're hearing this from an old soldier," he said. "I suppose you've got to *read* it to believe it, that's the new way. Maybe I'll write a book. I remember when the Chinks swarmed across the river down into Korea. That would make a book. Trouble is, they want philosophy in with the real action. I'd like to write it straight, just how it happened, but I can see the rejection slips already. That's the problem, you gotta knock the military to get a book published. God, I could write a book."

"Sir, the reason I'm here—I'm disturbed about the Vietnam war. I think it's, you know, wrong. I'm worried about having to—"

"I know how it is, trooper, we all get scared. Once you're in the thick of it, though, don't worry, you stop being scared. Christ, it's exhilarating sometimes. Man against man, only one wins. And if you lose, you lose big. But there's not a soldier, unless he's a liar, who doesn't admit he gets scared sometimes. Mostly it's before the battles and after them. That's how it was with me. Christ, all us officers would sit around and drink and joke about getting our asses creamed, but we were scared, even the officers. See, we're human."

He leaned forward and smiled for the first time. He'd made his big point.

I smiled and nodded.

The interview had climaxed.

"Well, does that help, trooper? I should talk with you men more often, but you know how it is. A lot of problems and misunderstandings could be avoided. If any other things that crop up—bad food, lousy mail —just let me know. I like to think my men can see me whenever there are problems. You're dismissed."

During advanced infantry training we were granted some after-hours freedom. There were three places on the fort to pass this time. One was the movie house. *Barbarella* ran for three weeks straight. One was the doughnut shop. The doughnuts were cheap and hot, and I spent money and time in one of the booths. The best place was the library. It was small, almost always empty, and the place had some good books.

I kept my escape plans folded up in my wallet. With spot inspections, they weren't safe in the wall lockers. I found a secluded table in the library and spent one or two hours a day working on the plan. Back issues of the major news magazines helped fill in details about Swedish immigration laws. I took notes on Swedish history, culture, and politics. I started to learn the language, words for food, drink, army, and deserter. The encyclopedia helped, and I learned the names of the major Swedish cities, names of rivers and lakes and ports.

On Sundays I didn't take the usual bus ride into Seattle or Tacoma. Instead, I wrote letters to my family, a teacher, and some friends, trying to explain my position. The letters to hometown America were tough to write. Worse to read, of course. I explained the grounds for my desertion in the letters, and I talked about the problems of conscience in participating in the war. Mostly, though, I tried to say how difficult it is to embarrass people you love. I hid the letters and decided to mail them from Canada, my first stop.

A week or two before Christmas I had enough money, the right documents, and a final plan. I was sick with bronchitis, but the little spurts of nausea and coughing pushed me on. It was a symptom of another disease, and there was absolutely no doubt about the cure. I was given a weekend pass.

The bus ride into Seattle was a jolt. It was a Friday evening, cold as ever, and a little snow had replaced the rain. The inside of the Greyhound was unlighted, except for cigarette glows. Everyone was in uniform, even the bus driver, and green berets jutted up here and there over the high-backed seats. The officers wore their Nazi-styled billed caps and dress greens and medals.

I was scared. I was also a little sick. My throat was filled with phlegm. Nausea flirted up and down my belly.

A lieutenant sat beside me, and he asked if I were heading home for Christmas. I said, "No sir, just a pass."

"Gonna hit Seattle, huh? Not a bad place. Better than Nam, that's for sure."

"Ah, you've been to Nam?"

"Nope, I'm just going. Day after tomorrow. The bastards wouldn't hold it till after the holiday."

"Too bad."

"What's your MOS?" the lieutenant asked.

"Infantry."

"Drafted, I'll bet. Me too. I signed up for OCS. Didn't really want to be an officer, but at least it delayed Nam for a while. Hell, I almost thought they forgot about me. In another month—this February—I could have been in Germany. My whole unit's going there."

"You got screwed, sir."

"Yeah," he said. "But I guess that's what I've been training for. Actually, I sort of want to try out all the stuff I've learned. I think I'm better than those dinks."

The Greyhound turned out of the fort. There is a long highway, three and four lanes, and it takes you through the black forests straight into Seattle. My head hurt, and I leaned back and sort of fell asleep, not a deep sleep, but enough to hallucinate. I dreamed that my old basic drill sergeant, Blyton, was sitting there beside me, grinning and telling me I was doomed. "I'll have you in the stockade, in chains, with bread and water. My man never gets away."

In Seattle, the depot was jammed full of MP's and cops. I went into the men's room and stripped. I stuffed my greens into the black AWOL bag and changed into slacks and a shirt. No one said a word.

I found a cheap hotel where I could hole up and think the whole thing through for one final night. An old lady at the desk handed me a key without a glance. The *Seattle Times* sports page was spread out in front of her. Like a gentleman, I said good evening. She muttered good evening. I dropped the bag onto my bed, then wandered out of the hotel and toward the docks. I found a sailor and asked for a good place to eat. "Over yonder," he said. "Good fish, and cheap. You ain't got a dime?" I had clam chowder, which

71

helped my headache; then I went to a telephone booth and called a taxi and took it to the University of Washington.

I walked into a sorority house and rang a button. A girl came down in jeans. Black hair, and blue-rimmed glasses. I told her I was from Minnesota, that one of my fraternity friends there had said I might find a date if I just rang for a girl in this house. She asked for my friend's name, and I manufactured one. She asked about the fraternity, and, not knowing any of the names, I said Phi Gamma Omega. She said she'd never heard of Phi Gamma Omega, but she crossed her arms and hooked one ankle around the other and seemed willing to talk.

"Actually," I said, "I'm not a sex maniac. I'm just visiting Seattle, and I didn't want to waste the night. Maybe a movie or something?"

"Jeez," the girl said. "You look like a pretty nice guy. But you know how it is, I have to study. Big exam tomorrow."

"Tomorrow's Saturday. You have classes on Saturday?"

"No, not really. The test's Monday. It just slipped out, I guess."

"Well," I said, "the truth is, I didn't think you'd want to go. But maybe you know somebody."

"Sorry. But it's just before Christmas break. We're having finals, you know, and all my friends are at the books." She smiled. "Besides, this is no way to conduct human relations."

So I left, embarrassed, and went to downtown Seattle. I walked around in the simmering red and gold neon light, past a theater showing *Finian's Rainbow*—". . . if I'm not near the girl that I love, I love the girl I'm near!"—and past another theater showing

The Graduate, which made me think about my college sweetheart. I walked along, whistling "Old Devil Moon" until my headache started again.

Farther up the street, toward the harbor, the lights faded. A prostitute hooked me with her umbrella and asked if I needed a date.

"No, thanks," I said. "I feel kind of sick tonight."

"Well, then, can you spare a buck or two?" she asked.

"Sorry. I really need the money. You don't know how much I need it."

I vomited in my hotel room. I fell asleep, awakened, slept again, awakened to hear it raining. I looked down at the street, and the snow was gone and it was all gray slush. I sat at the desk. The AWOL bag was ready to go, but I wasn't. I slept some more, dreaming, and when I awakened I vomited and saw it was getting light. I burned the letters to my family. I read the others and burned them, too. It was over. I simply couldn't bring myself to flee. Family, the home town, friends, history, tradition, fear, confusion, exile: I could not run. I went into the hallway and bought a Coke. When I finished it I felt better, clearer-headed, and burned the plans. I was a coward. I was sick.

All day Saturday I was sick. And restless and hopeless. On Sunday morning I caught a bus to the fort. I went to the library and read, ate a doughnut in the doughnut shop, and went on back to the barracks. The rest of the men were loud coming in from pass, drunk and squabbling and howling and talking about Christmas. There was just no place to be alone.

VII

Arrival

First there is some mist. Then, when the plane begins
its descent, there are pale gray mountains. The plane
slides down, and the mountains darken and take on
a sinister cragginess. You see the outlines of crevices,
and you consider whether, of all the places opening
up below, you might finally walk to *that* spot and die.
Or that spot, or that spot. In the far distance are green
patches, the sea is below, a stretch of sand winds along
the coast. Two hundred men draw their breath. You
feel dread. But it is senseless to let it go too far, so
you joke: there are only 365 days to go. The stewardess
wishes you luck over the loudspeaker. At the door she
gives out some kisses, mainly to the extroverts.

From Cam Ranh Bay another plane takes you to
Chu Lai, a big base to the south of Danang, headquarters for the Americal Division. You spend a week
there, in a place called the Combat Center. It's a
resortlike place, tucked in alongside the South China
Sea, complete with sand and native girls and a miniature golf course and floor shows with every variety of
the grinding female pelvis. There beside the sea you
get your now-or-never training. You pitch hand grenades, practice walking through mine fields, learn to
use a minesweeper. Mostly, though, you wonder about
dying. You wonder how it feels, what it looks like in-

74

side you. Sometimes you stop, and your body tingles. You feel your blood and nerves working. At night you sit on the beach and watch fire fights off where the war is being fought. There are movies at night, and a place to buy beer. Carefully, you mark six days off your pocket calendar; you start a journal, vaguely hoping it will never be read.

Arriving in Vietnam as a foot soldier is much like arriving at boot camp as a recruit. Things are new, and you ascribe evil to the simplest physical objects: You see red in the sand, swarms of angels and avatars in the sky, pity in the eyes of the chaplain, concealed anger in the eyes of the girls who sell you Coke. You are not sure how to conduct yourself—whether to show fear, to live secretly with it, to show resignation or disgust. You wish it were all over. You begin the countdown. You take the inky, mildew smell of Vietnam into your lungs.

After a week at the Combat Center, a truck took six of us down Highway One to a hill called LZ Gator.

A sergeant welcomed us, staring at us like he was buying meat, and he explained that LZ Gator was headquarters for the Fifth Battalion, Forty-Sixth Infantry, and that the place was our new home.

"But I don't want you guys getting too used to Gator," he said. "You won't be here long. You're gonna fill out some forms in a few minutes, then we'll get you all assigned to rifle companies, then you're going out to the boonies. Got it? Just like learning to swim. We just toss you in and let you hoof it and eat some C rations and get a little action under your belts. It's better that way than sitting around worrying about it.

"Okay, that's enough bullshit. Just don't get no illusions." He softened his voice a trifle. "Of course,

75

don't get too scared. We lose some men, sure, but it ain't near as bad as '66, believe me, I was in the Nam in '66, an' it was bad shit then, getting our butts kicked around. And this area—you guys lucked out a little, there's worse places in the Nam. We got mines, that's the big thing here, plenty of 'em. But this ain't the Delta, we ain't got many NVA, so you're lucky. We got some mines and some local VC, that's it. Anyhow, enough bullshit, like I say, it ain't all that bad. Okay, we got some personnel cards here, so fill 'em out, and we'll chow you down."

Then the battalion Re-Up NCO came along. "I seen some action. I got me two purple hearts, so listen up good. I'm not saying you're gonna get zapped out there. I made it. But you're gonna come motherfuckin' close, Jesus, you're gonna hear bullets tickling your asshole. And sure as I'm standing here, one or two of you men are gonna get your legs blown off. Or killed. One or two of you, it's gotta happen."

He paused and stared around like a salesman, from man to man, letting it sink in. "I'm just telling you the facts of life, I'm not trying to scare shit out of you. But you better sure as hell be scared, it's gotta happen. One or two of you men, your ass is grass.

"So—what can you do about it? Well, like Sarge says, you can be careful, you can watch for the mines and all that, and, who knows, you might come out looking like a rose. But careful guys get killed too. So what can you do about it then? Nothing. Except you can re-up."

The men looked at the ground and shuffled around grinning. "Sure, sure—I know. Nobody likes to re-up. But just think about it a second. Just say you do it— you take your burst of three years, starting today; three more years of army life. Then what? Well, I'll tell you what, it'll save your ass, that's what, it'll save your ass. You re-up and I can get you a job in Chu Lai. I got jobs for mechanics, typists, clerks, damn near anything you want, I got it. So you get your nice, safe rear job. You get some on-the-job training, the works. You get a skill. You sleep in a bed. Hell, you laugh, but you sleep in the goddamn monsoons for two months on end, you try that sometime, and you won't be laughing. So. You lose a little time to Uncle Sam. Big deal. You save your ass. So, I got my desk inside. If you come in and sign the papers—it'll take ten minutes—I'll have you on the first truck going back to Chu Lai, no shit. Anybody game?" No one budged, and he shrugged and went down to the mess hall.

LZ Gator seemed a safe place to be. You could see pieces of the ocean on clear days. A little village called Nuoc Mau was at the foot of the hill, filled with pleasant, smiling people, places to have your laundry done, a whorehouse. Except when on perimeter guard at night, everyone went about the fire base with unloaded weapons. The atmosphere was dull and hot, but there were movies and floor shows and sheds-ful of beer.

I was assigned to Alpha Company.

"Shit, you poor sonofabitch," the mail clerk said, grinning. "Shit. How many days you got left in Nam? 358, right? 357? Shit. You poor mother. I got twenty-three days left, twenty-three days, and I'm sorry but I'm gone! Gone! I'm so short I need a step ladder to hand out mail. What's your name?"

The mail clerk shook hands with me. "Well, at least you're a lucky sonofabitch. Irish guys never get wasted, not in Alpha. Blacks and spics get wasted, but you micks make it every goddamn time. Hell, I'm black

77

as the colonel's shoe polish, so you can bet your ass I'm not safe till that ol' freedom bird lands me back in Seattle. Twenty-three days, you poor mother."

He took me to the first sergeant. The first sergeant said to forget all the bullshit about going straight out to the field. He lounged in front of a fan, dressed in his underwear (dyed green, apparently to camouflage him from some incredibly sneaky VC), and he waved a beer at me. "Shit, O'Brien, take it easy. Alpha's a good square-shooting company, so don't sweat it. Keep your nose clean and I'll just keep you here on Gator till the company comes back for a break. No sense sending you out there now, they're coming in to Gator day after tomorrow." He curled his toe around a cord and pulled the fan closer. "Go see a movie tonight, get a beer or something."

He assigned me to the third platoon and hollered at the supply sergeant to issue me some gear. The supply sergeant hollered back for him to go to hell, and they laughed, and I got a rifle and ammunition and a helmet, camouflage cover, poncho, poncho liner, back pack, clean clothes, and a box of cigarettes and candy. Then it got dark, and I watched Elvira Madigan and her friend romp through all the colors, get hungry, get desperate, and stupidly—so stupidly that you could only pity their need for common sense—end their lives. The guy, Elvira's lover, was a deserter. You had the impression he deserted for an ideal of love and butter-flies, balmy days and the simple life, and that when he saw he couldn't have it, not even with blond and blue-eyed Elvira, he decided he could *never* have it. But, Jesus, to kill because of hunger, for fear to hold a menial job. Disgusted, I went off to an empty bar-racks and pushed some M-16 ammo and hand gre-nades off my cot and went to sleep.

In two days Alpha Company came to LZ Gator. They were dirty, loud, coarse, intent on getting drunk, happy, curt, and not interested in saying much to me. They drank through the afternoon and into the night. There was a fight that ended in more beer, they smoked some dope, they started sleeping or passed out around midnight.

At one or two in the morning—at first I thought I was dreaming, then I thought it was nothing serious—explosions popped somewhere outside the barracks. The first sergeant came through the barracks with a flashlight. "Jesus," he hollered. "Get the hell out of here! We're being hit! Wake up!"

I scrambled for a helmet for my head. For an armored vest. For my boots, for my rifle, for my ammo.

It was pitch dark. The explosions continued to pop; it seemed a long distance away.

I went outside. The base was lit up by flares, and the mortar pits were firing rounds out into the paddies. I hid behind a metal shed they kept the beer in.

No one else came out of the barracks. I waited, and finally one man ambled out, holding a beer. Then another man, holding a beer.

They sat on some sandbags in their underwear, drinking the beer and laughing, pointing out at the paddies and watching our mortar rounds land.

Later two or three more men straggled out. No helmets, no weapons. They laughed and joked and drank. The first sergeant started shouting. But the men just giggled and sat on sandbags in their underwear.

Enemy rounds crashed in. The earth split. Most of Alpha Company slept.

A lieutenant came by. He told the men to get their gear together, but no one moved, and he walked away.

Then some of the men spotted the flash of an enemy mortar tube.

They set up a machine gun and fired out at it, over the heads of everyone in the fire base.

In seconds the enemy tube flashed again. The wind whistled, and the round dug into a road twenty feet from my beer shed. Shrapnel slammed into the beer shed. I hugged the Bud and Black Label, panting, no thoughts.

Charlie was zeroing in on their machine gun, and everyone scattered, and the next round slammed down even closer. More giggling and hooting.

The lieutenant hurried back. He argued with a platoon sergeant, but this time the lieutenant was firm. He ordered us to double-time out to the perimeter. Muttering about how the company needed a rest and that this had turned into one hell of a rest and that they'd rather be out in the boonies, the men put on helmets and took up their rifles and followed the lieutenant past the mess hall and out to the perimeter.

Three of the men refused and went into the barracks and went to sleep.

Out on the perimeter, there were two dead GI's. Fifty-caliber machine guns fired out into the paddies, and the sky was filled with flares. Two or three of our men, forgetting about the war, went off to chase parachutes blowing around the bunkers. The chutes came from the flares, and they made good souvenirs.

In the morning the first sergeant roused us out of bed, and we swept the fire base for bodies. Eight dead VC were lying about. One was crouched beside a roll of barbed wire, the top of his head resting on the ground like he was ready to do a somersault. A squad of men was detailed to throw the corpses into a truck.

80

They wore gloves and didn't like the job, but they joked. The rest of us walked into the rice paddy and followed a tracker dog out toward the VC mortar positions. From there the dog took us into a village, but there was nothing to see but some children and women. We walked around until noon. Then the lieutenant turned us around, and we were back at LZ Gator in time for chow.

"Those poor motherfuckin' dinks," the Kid said while we were filling sandbags in the afternoon. "They should know better than to test Alpha Company. They just know, they *ought* to know anyhow, it's like tryin' to attack the Pentagon! Old Alpha comes in, an' there ain't a chance in hell for 'em, they ought to know *that,* for Christ's sake. Eight to two, they lost six more than we did." The Kid was only eighteen, but everyone said to look out for him, he was the best damn shot in the battalion with an M-79.

"Actually," the Kid said, "those two guys weren't even from Alpha. The two dead GI's. They were with Charlie Company or something, I don't know. Stupid dinks should know better." He flashed a buck-toothed smile and jerked his eyebrows up and down and winked.

Wolf said: "Look, FNG, I don't want to scare you—nobody's trying to scare you—but that stuff last night wasn't *shit!* Last night was a lark. Wait'll you see some really *bad* shit. That was a picnic last night. I almost slept through it." I wondered what an FNG was. No one told me until I asked.

"You bullshitter, Wolf. It's never any fun." The Kid heaved a shovelful of sand at Wolf's feet. "Except for me maybe. I'm charmed, nothing'll get me. Ol' Buddy Wolf's a good bullshitter, he'll bullshit you till you think he knows his ass from his elbow."

"Okay, FNG, don't listen to me, ask Buddy Barker. Buddy Barker, you tell him last night was a lark. Right? We got mortars and wire and bunkers and arty and, shit, what the hell else you want? You want a damn H bomb?"

"Good idea," Kid said.

But Buddy Barker agreed it had been a lark. He filled a sandbag and threw it onto a truck and sat down and read a comic. Buddy Wolf filled two more bags and sat down with Buddy Barker and called him a lazy bastard. While Kid and I filled more bags, Wolf and Barker read comics and played a game called "Name the Gang." Wolf named a rock song and Barker named the group who made it big. Wolf won 10 to 2. I asked the Kid how many Alpha men had been killed lately, and the Kid shrugged and said a couple. So I asked how many had been wounded, and without looking up, he said a few. I asked how bad the AO was, how soon you could land a rear job, if the platoon leader were gung-ho, if Kid had ever been wounded, and the Kid just grinned and gave flippant, smiling, say-nothing answers. He said it was best not to worry.

VIII

Alpha Company

The first month with Alpha Company was a peculiar time. It was mostly a vacation. We wandered up and down the beaches outside Chu Lai, pulling security patrols and a very few night ambushes. It was an infantryman's dream. There were no VC, no mines, sunny days, warm seas to swim in, daily resupplies of milk and beer. We were a traveling circus. A caravan of local children and women followed us from one stretch of sand to the next, peddling Coke and dirty pictures, cleaning our weapons for a can of C rations. During the days we played football. Two or three lovers lounged under their ponchos with Vietnamese girls. They flirted, and there were some jealousies and hurt feelings. When we moved to a new position, our column stretched out for a quarter-mile, filled with soldiers and prostitutes and girls carrying bags of Coke and children carrying our packs and sometimes even our rifles. At dusk the children dug our foxholes. Each GI had his personal mascot, his valet. My own helper was a little guy called Champion. He was ten years old, perhaps even younger, but he knew how to disassemble and clean my rifle, and he knew how to give a back rub.

During the first month, I learned that FNG meant "fuckin new guy," and that I would be one until the

Combat Center's next shipment arrived. I learned that GI's in the field can be as lazy and careless and stupid as GI's anywhere. They don't wear helmets and armored vests unless an officer insists; they fall asleep on guard, and for the most part, no one really cares; they throw away or bury ammunition if it gets heavy and hot. I learned that REMF means "rear echelon motherfucker"; that a man is getting "Short" after his third or fourth month; that a hand grenade is really a "frag"; that one bullet is all it takes and that "you never hear the shot that gets you"; that no one in Alpha Company gave a damn about the causes or purposes of their war: It is about "dinks and slopes," and the idea is simply to kill them or avoid them. Except that in Alpha you don't kill a man, you "waste" him. You don't get mangled by a mine, you get "fucked up." You don't call a man by his first name—he's the Kid or the Water Buffalo, Buddy Wolf or Buddy Barker or Buddy Barney, or if the fellow is bland or disliked, he's just Smith or Jones or Rodríguez. The NCO's who go through a crash two-month program to earn their stripes are called "Instant NCO's"; hence the platoon's squad leaders were named Ready Whip, Nestle's Quick, and Shake and Bake. And when two of them—Tom and Arnold—were killed two months later, the tragedy was somehow lessened and depersonalized by telling ourselves that ol' Ready Whip and Quick got themselves wasted by the slopes. There was Cop—an Irish fellow who wanted to join the police force in Danbury, Connecticut—and Reno and the Wop and the College Joe. You can go through a year in Vietnam and live with a platoon of sixty or seventy people, some going and some coming, and you can leave without knowing more than a dozen complete names, not that it matters.

Mad Mark was the platoon leader, a first lieutenant and a Green Beret. It was hard to tell if the name or the reason for the name came first. The madness in Mad Mark, at any rate, was not a hysterical, crazy, into-the-brink, to-the-fore madness. Rather, he was insanely calm. He never showed fear. He was a professional soldier, an ideal leader of men in the field. It was that kind of madness, the perfect guardian for the Platonic Republic. His attitude and manner were those of a CIA operative. A lover of stealth. A pro, a hired hand. It was his manner, and he cultivated it. He walked with a lanky, easy, silent, fearless stride. He wore tiger fatigues, not for their camouflage but for their look. He carried a shotgun—a weapon I'd thought was outlawed in international war—and the shotgun itself was a measure of his professionalism, for to use it effectively requires an exact blend of courage and skill and self-confidence. The weapon is neither accurate nor lethal at much over fifty yards. So it shows the skill of the carrier, a man who must work his way close enough to the prey to make a shot, close enough to see the enemy's eyes and the tone of his skin. To get that close requires courage and confidence. The shotgun is not an automatic weapon. You must hit once, on the first shot, and the hit must kill. Mad Mark once said that after the war and in the absence of other U.S. wars he might try the mercenary's life in Africa.

He did not yearn for battle. But neither was he concerned about the prospect. Throughout the first month, vacationing on the safe beaches, he did precisely what the mission called for: a few patrols, a few ambushes, staying ready to react, watching for signs of a rocket attack on Chu Lai. But he did not take the mission to excess. Mad Mark was not a fanatic.

He was not gung-ho, not a man in search of a fight. It was more or less an Aristotelian ethic that Mad Mark practiced: making war is a necessary and natural profession. It is natural, but it is only a profession, not a crusade: "Hunting is a part of that art; and hunting might be practiced—not only against wild animals, but also against human beings who are intended by nature to be ruled by others and refuse to obey that intention—because war of this order is naturally just." And, like Aristotle, Mad Mark believed in and practiced the virtue of moderation; he did what was necessary in war, necessary for an officer and platoon leader in war; he did no more or less.

He lounged with us during the hot days, he led a few patrols and ambushes, he flirted with the girls in our caravan, and, with a concern for only the basics of discipline, he allowed us to enjoy the holiday. Lying in the shade with the children, we learned a little Vietnamese, and they learned words like "mother-fucker" and "gook" and "dink" and "tit." Like going to school.

It was not a bad war until we sent a night patrol into a village called Tri Binh 4. Mad Mark led it, taking only his shotgun and five other men. They'd been gone for an hour. Then came a burst of fire and a radio call that they'd opened up on some VC smoking and talking by a well. In ten minutes they were out of the hamlet and back with the platoon.

The Kid was ecstatic. "Christ! They were right out there, right in the open, right in the middle of the ville, in a little clearing, just sitting on their asses! Shit, I almost shit! Ten of 'em, just sitting there. Jesus, we gave 'em hell. Damn, we gave it to 'em!" His face was on fire, his teeth were flashing, he was

86

grinning himself out of his skin. He paced back and forth, wanting to burst.

"Jesus," he said. "Show 'em the ear we got! Let's see the ear!"

Someone turned on a flashlight.

Mad Mark sat cross-legged and unwrapped a bundle of cloth and dangled a hunk of brown, fresh human ear under the yellow beam of light. Someone giggled. The ear was clean of blood. It dripped with a little water, as if coming out of a bathtub. Part of the upper lobe was gone. A band of skin flopped away from the ear, at the place where the ear had been held to a man's head. It looked alive. It looked like it would move in Mad Mark's hands, as if it might make a squirm for freedom. It had the texture of a hunk of elastic.

"Christ, Mad Mark just went up and sliced it off the dead dink! No wonder he's Mad Mark. Like he was cuttin' sausages or something."

"What you gonna do with it? Why don't you *eat* it, Mad Mark?"

"Bullshit, who's gonna eat a goddamn dink? I eat women, not dead dinks."

Kid laughed. "We got some money off the gook, too. A whole shitload."

One of the men pulled out a roll of greasy piasters. The members of the patrol split it up and pocketed it; then they passed the ear around for everyone to fondle.

Mad Mark called in gunships. For an hour the helicopters strafed and rocketed Tri Binh 4. The sky and the trees and the hillsides were lighted up by spotlights and tracers and fires. From our position we could smell smoke coming from the village. We heard cattle and chickens and dogs dying. At two in the

87

morning we started to sleep, one man at a time. Tri Binh 4 turned curiously quiet. Smoke continued to billow over to our position all night, and when I awakened every hour, it was the first thing to sense and to remind me of the ear. In the morning another patrol was sent into the village. The dead VC soldier was still there, stretched out on his back with his eyes closed and his arms folded and his head cocked to one side so that you could not see where the ear was gone. Little fires burned in some of the huts. Dead animals lay about. There were no people. We searched Tri Binh 4, then burned most of it down.

IX

Ambush

"Tonight," Mad Mark said quietly, "we are sending out an ambush."

It was near dusk, and the lieutenant had his map spread out in the dirt in front of a foxhole. His squad leaders were grouped in a circle around him, watching where he drew X's, taking notes. Mad Mark pointed at a spot on the map, circled it, and said, "We'll be bushing this trail junction. Headquarters has some pretty good intelligence that Charlie's in the neighborhood. Maybe we'll nail him this time."

He drew two red lines on the map. "First squad will set up along this paddy dike. Make sure the grenade launchers and machine guns aren't bunched together. Okay, Second Squad lines up along this hedgerow. That way we form an L. We get Charlie coming either way. Third and Fourth squads stay here tonight. I'll lead the ambush myself."

He asked if there were questions, but the squad leaders were all experienced, and no one said anything.

"Okay, good enough. We move out at midnight—maybe a little after. Make sure you bring enough Claymores. And for Christ's sake, don't forget the firing devices. Also, tell every man to carry a couple of grenades. No freeloading. Let's get some kills."

The night turned into the purest earthly black, no stars and no moon. We sat around our foxholes in small groups, some of us muttering that it was bad luck to send out ambushes on nights as dark as this one. Often we had simply faked the whole thing, calling in the ambush coordinates to headquarters and then forgetting it. But Mad Mark apparently wanted to give it a try this time, and there was nothing to do about it. At midnight the squad leaders began moving from foxhole to foxhole, rousing men out. We hung grenades from our belts. We threw our helmets into foxholes—they were a hindrance at night, distorting hearing, too heavy, and, if it came to a fire fight, they made it hard to shoot straight. Instead we put on bush hats or went bareheaded. Every third man picked up a Claymore mine. We wiped dirt off our rifles, took a drink of water, urinated in the weeds, then lay on our backs to wait.

"The wait," Chip murmured. "I hate the wait, seeing it get dark, knowing I got to go out. Don't want to get killed in the dark."

When Mad Mark moved us out of the perimeter and into the darkness, the air was heavy. There were none of the sounds of nature. No birds, no wind, no rain, no grass rustling, no crickets. We moved through the quiet. Metal clanging, canteens bouncing, twigs splintering and hollering out our names, water sloshing, we stepped like giants through the night. Mad Mark stopped us. He spoke to two or three men at a time, and when it was my turn he whispered that we must hold the noise down, that he, at least, didn't want to die that night. It did no good.

Mad Mark led us across a rice paddy and onto a narrow, winding dirt road. The road circled a village. A dog barked. Voices spoke urgently inside the huts, perhaps parents warning children to stay down, sensing the same certain danger which numbed all twenty of us, the intruders. We circled the village and left it. The dog's barking lasted for twenty minutes, echoing out over the paddies and following us as we closed in on the trail junction.

One of the most persistent and appalling thoughts that lumbers through your mind as you walk through Vietnam at night is the fear of getting lost, of becoming detached from the others, of spending the night alone in that frightening and haunted countryside. It was dark. We walked in a single file, perhaps three yards apart. Mad Mark took us along a crazy, wavering course. We veered off the road, through clumps of trees, through tangles of bamboo and grass, zigzagging through graveyards of dead Vietnamese who lay there under conical mounds of dirt and clay. The man to the front and the man to the rear were the only holds on security and sanity. We followed the man in front like a blind man after his dog; we prayed that the man had not lost *his* way, that he hadn't lost contact with the man to his front. We tensed our eyeballs, peered straight ahead. We hurt ourselves staring. We strained. We dared not look away for fear the man leading us might fade and turn into shadow. Sometimes, when the dark closed in, we reached out to him, touched his shirt.

The man to the front is civilization. He is the United States of America and every friend you have ever known; he is Erik and blond girls and a mother and a father. He is your life. And, for the man stumbling along behind you, you alone are his torch.

The pace was slow, and the march brought back thoughts of basic training. I thought of the song about the Viet Cong: "Vietnam, Vietnam, every night while you're sleepin' Charlie Cong comes a-creepin' all around." I thought of the *Legend of Sleepy Hollow*, of imminent violence and guileless, gentle Ichabod Crane. Which turn of the road, which threatening shadow of a tree held his nightmare in hiding? I remembered a dream I'd had as a kid, a fourteen-year-old sleeping in southern Minnesota. It was the only dream I have ever remembered in detail. I was in prison. It was somewhere in a very black and evil land. The prison was a hole in a mountain. During the days, swarthy-faced, moustached captors worked us like slaves in coal mines. At night they locked us behind rocks. They had whips and guns, and they used them on us at pleasure. The mountain dungeon was musty. Suddenly we were free, escaping, scrambling out of the cave. Searchlights and sirens and machine-gun fire pierced the night, cutting us down. Men were bellowing. It rained. It was a medium drizzle bringing out a musty smell of sedge and salamanders. I raced through the night, my heart bloated and aching. I fell. Behind me there were torches blazing and the shouts of the swarthy-faced pursuers. I plunged into a forest. I ran and finally came out of the trees and made my way to the top of a mountain. I lay there. The torches and noise and gunfire were gone. I looked into the valley below me, and a carnival was there. A beautiful woman, covered with feathers and tan skin, was charming snakes. With her stick she prodded the creatures, making them dance and writhe and perform. I hollered down to her, "Which way to freedom? Which way home?" She was a mile away, but she lifted her stick and pointed the way down a road. I loved the woman, snakes and stick and tanned skin. I followed the road, the rain became heavier, I whistled and felt happy and in love. The rain stopped. The road opened to a clearing in a dark forest. The woman was there, beads of water scattered on her arms and thighs. Her arm was around a swarthy, moustached captor, and she was laughing and pointing her stick at me. The captor embraced her, and together they took me away. Back to prison. That was the dream. I was thinking of that dream as we walked along, finally coming on the trail junction.

Mad Mark dispersed us along the two trails, setting us up in the L-shaped formation he'd mapped out back at camp.

He gave me a Claymore and pointed at a spot along the east-west trail. I felt brave and silly walking out onto the dark road. The deadly device worked just as it had during training. I inserted the blasting cap in a hole on top of the mine. I opened up the mine's little metal legs and plugged them into the dirt, aiming the concave face out toward the middle of the junction. I crept back to the hedgerow, unwinding the wire behind me; I plugged the wire into its firing device, put the thing on safety, and waited. It would be Ichabod's revenge.

We were paired into ten teams of two men each. One man in each team would sleep while the other watched the road: an hour on and an hour off until daybreak.

My partner was a kid we called Reno. His real name was Jim or something. He probably chose Reno as a nickname over such others as Ringo, the Sunset Kid, and Flash. He was a squad leader, and I didn't care for him. He liked his job too well.

He gave me his watch, and he rolled onto his back. He pulled his hat down and was asleep. He slept quietly. At least that was in his favor.

Watching the road was not an easy thing. The

hedgerow was thick. I tried it on my knees, but that didn't give enough elevation. I tried standing, but there is a certain horrible sensation that comes from standing on your feet on an ambush. Finally I stooped and squatted down. It hurt the thighs, but the road was visible, and it would be tough to fall asleep that way.

I took hold of the Claymore's firing device, testing its feel. It fit my hand well. I flicked the safety back and forth to be sure it wouldn't jam. I was jittery. What to do? I toyed with my M-16, patting the magazine, rubbing the trigger. Would the weapon work when the moment came? I pictured myself desperately yanking at that trigger, over and over, bawling, screaming, but the gun wouldn't fire.

Other thoughts. Memories, fantasies. I imagined that the twenty of us had suddenly become the objects of this night's hunt, that we were fooling ourselves to think that we remained the hunters. There we lay, twenty lonely GI's without foxholes or barbed wire or a perimeter for protection. Ten of us were sleeping. The others gazed stupidly in one direction, out at the trail junction, as if the war gods had it arranged that the Viet Cong should trot down before our gunsights like drugged turkeys. I remembered an old Daffy Duck movie cartoon. A well-equipped hunter—red cap, ten-gauge shotgun, sacked lunch—lies in wait behind an elaborate blind, chortling at the cleverness of his concealment. And all the while ol' Daffy is prancing up from behind the doomed fellow, sledgehammer and sticks of red dynamite at the ready. A whole theater full of preadolescent sadists ripped into laughter when Daffy sent the hunter to Never-Never Land, abroad a gratifying shock wave. I led the laughter. I'd always favored the quarry over the hunter. It seemed only fair.

I glanced backward. Only trees and shadows.

I woke Reno, gave him the wristwatch, and curled up around my rifle.

It was cold. The ground was wet.

Reno slapped a mosquito and sat cross-legged, staring dead into a clump of bushes. He was a veteran, I thought. He knew what he was doing. Immediately, incredibly, I fell into a peaceful, heavy sleep.

Reno awakened me. My fatigues were drenched, a soggy web. It was drizzling and it was cold. I asked Reno for the wristwatch. It was three-ten. Reno had cheated by a few minutes. My sleep should have ended at three-twenty, but he was a squad leader, and there wasn't anything to say about it. He grinned. "Don't get too wet, New Guy," he said, not bothering to whisper. "You catch pneumonia, we'll have to ship you to the rear. I bet you'd hate that." He lit a cigarette, cupping it in his palm. That was stupid and against the rules, but I couldn't decide if it was more cowardly to tell him to put it out or to keep quiet and hope he'd die of lung cancer. The rain finally extinguished the cigarette, and Reno rolled around on the ground until he was asleep.

I passed the hour counting up the number of days I had left in Vietnam. I figured it out by months, weeks, and hours. I thought about a girl. It was hopeless, of course, but I tried to visualize her face. Only words would come in my mind. One word was "smile," and I tacked on the adjective "intriguing" to make it more personal. I thought of the word "hair" and modified it with the words "thick" and "sandy," not sure if they were accurate anymore, and then a whole string of words popped in—"mysterious," "Magdalen," "Eternal" as a modifier. I tried fitting the words together into a picture, and I tried closing my eyes, first taking a long look down the road. I tried forcing out the memory of the girl, tried placing her in situations, tried reciting the Auden poem in a very brave whisper. For all this, I could not see her. When I muttered the word "hair," I could see her hair plainly enough. When I said "eyes," I would be looking smack into a set of smiling blue irises, and they were hers, no doubt. But if I uttered the word "face" or tried to squeeze out a picture of the girl herself, all there was to see was the word "face" or the word "eye," printed out before me. It was like asking a computer to see for me. And I was learning that no weight of letters and remembering and wishing and hoping is the same as a touch on temporary, mortgaged lands.

I spent some time thinking about the things I would do after Vietnam—after the first sergeants and rifles were out of my life. I made a long list. I would write about the army. Expose the brutality and injustice and stupidity and arrogance of wars and men who fight in them. Get even with some people. Mark out the evil in my drill sergeants so vividly that they would go to hell lamenting the day they tangled with Private O'Brien. I would expose the carelessness with which people like Reno played with my life. I would crusade against this war, and if, when I was released, I would find other wars, I would work to discover whether they were just and necessary, and if I found they were not, I would have another crusade. I wondered how writers such as Hemingway and Pyle could write so accurately and movingly about war without also writing about the rightness of their wars. I remembered one of Hemingway's stories. It was about a battle in World War I, about the hideous deaths of tides of human beings, swarming into the fight, engaging under the sun, and ebbing away again into two piles, friend and foe. I wondered why he did not care to talk about the thoughts those men must have had. Certainly those suffering and scared human beings must have wondered if their cause was worthy. The men in war novels and stories and reportage seem to come off the typewriter as men resigned to bullets and brawn. Hemingway's soldiers especially. They are cynics. Not quite nihilists, of course, for that would doom them in the reader's eye. But what about the people who are persuaded that their battle is not only futile but also dead wrong? What about the con-scripted Nazi?

I made plans to travel. I thought of buying or rent-ing a secondhand boat and with six or seven friends sailing the seas from Australia to Lisbon, then to the Côte d'Azur, Sicily, and to an island called Paros in the Aegean. Perhaps I might rent a cottage in Austria, perhaps near a town called Freistadt just across the Czechoslovakian border. Freistadt would be the ideal place. The mountains were formidable, the air was clean, the town had a dry moat around it, the beer was the best in the world, the girls were not communists, and they had blue eyes and blond hair and big bosoms. There would be skiing in the winter and hiking and swimming in the summer. I would sleep alone when I wanted to, not in a barracks and not along a trail junction with nineteen GI's.

The thought of Freistadt, Austria, turned me to thinking about Prague, Czechoslovakia, where I'd spent a summer trying to study. I remembered an eve-ning in July of 1967. I'd been drinking beer with a young Czech student, an economics specialist. Walk-ing back from the *hostinec,* the fellow pointed out a poster that covered three square feet on a cement wall. The poster depicted three terrified Vietnamese girls.

They were running from the bombs of an American B-52 bomber. In the background, a North Vietnamese antiaircraft gun was blasting the planes with red fire. A clenched fist in the foreground.

The Czech asked what I thought of it. I told him I was ambivalent. I didn't know. Perhaps the bombs were falling for good reason.

He smiled. "I have an invitation to extend, a proposition for you. If you find it distasteful, just say so, but as an interested bystander I hope you'll accept. You see, my roommate is from North Vietnam. He studies economics here at the university. I wonder if you'd like to talk with him tonight." He chuckled. "Perhaps you two can negotiate a settlement, who knows."

It was a three-hour conversation. With my Czech friend helping with the translation, we carried on in French, Czech, German, and English. The fellow was cordial, a short and reserved man who told me his name was Li and offered me a seat on his bed. I asked if he thought Americans were evil, and he thought awhile before he said no. He asked me the same question and I said no, quickly. I asked if the North Vietnamese were not the aggressors in the war. He laughed and stated that of course the opposite was the case. They were defending Vietnam from American aggression. I asked if the North Vietnamese were not sending troops to the South in order to establish a communist regime in Saigon, and he laughed again, nervously, and informed me that to speak of a divided Vietnam was historically and politically incorrect. I asked Li if he believed that President Johnson was an evil man, another Hitler. Personally, he said, he didn't believe so. Johnson was misguided and wrong. But he added that most North Vietnamese were not so lenient.

"What else can they think when they see your airplanes killing people? They put the blame on the man who orders the flights."

We talked about democracy and totalitarianism, and the fellow argued that the government in Hanoi could be considered a wartime democracy. Stability, he said, was essential. We argued some about that, and my Czech friend joined in, taking my side.

When I left him, Li shook my hand and told me he was a lieutenant in the North Vietnamese Army. He hoped we would not meet again. That was in 1967.

I roused Reno out for the final watch. It was four-thirty, and the sky was lighting up and the worst was over. Reno lay on his back. His eyes were barely slit, and there was no way to be sure he was awake. I nudged him again, and he told me to relax and go to sleep. I put the Claymore firing device beside him, brushed his foot a little as I lay down, and closed my eyes. I was nearly asleep when I remembered the wrist-watch. I sat up and handed it out toward him. He was wheezing, sound asleep. I kicked him, and he sat up, lit a cigarette, took the wristwatch, and sat there in a daze, rocking on his haunches and staring at his clump of bushes.

An hour later, when Mad Mark hollered at us to saddle up and move out, Reno was on his stomach and wheezing. He was a seasoned American soldier, a combat veteran, a squad leader.

Not every ambush was so uneventful. Sometimes we found Charlie, sometimes it was the other way.

In the month of May, we broke camp at three in the morning, Captain Johansen leading three platoons on a ghostly, moonlit march to a village in the vicinity of the My Lai's. Johansen deployed the platoons in a broad circle around the village, forming a loose cordon. The idea was to gun down the Viet Cong as they left the ville before daybreak—intelligence had it that some sort of VC meeting was in progress. If no one exited by daybreak, the Third Platoon would sweep the village, driving the enemy into the rest of us.

Alpha Company pulled it off like professionals.

We were quiet, the cordon was drawn quickly, securely. I carried Captain Johansen's radio, and along with him, an artillery forward observer, and three other RTO's, we grouped along a paddy dike outside the village. Captain Johansen directed things by radio.

In less than an hour the Second Platoon opened up on four VC leaving by a north-south trail. Seconds later, more gunfire. Third Platoon was engaged.

Second Platoon called in again, confirming a kill. The stars were out. The Southern Cross was up there, smiling down on Alpha Company.

The artillery officer got busy, calling back to the rear, preparing the big guns for a turkey shoot, rapidly reading off grid coordinates, excited that we'd finally found the enemy.

Johansen was happy. He'd lost many men to the Forty-eighth Viet Cong Battalion. He was getting his revenge.

Rodríguez, one of the RTO's, suddenly uttered something in Spanish, changed it to English, and pointed out to our front. Three silhouettes were tiptoeing out of the hamlet. They were twenty yards away, crouched over, their shoulders hunched forward.

It was the first and only time I would ever see the living enemy, the men intent on killing me. Johansen whispered, "Aim low—when you miss, it's because you're shooting over the target."

We stood straight up, in a row, as if it were a contest.

I confronted the profile of a human being through my sight. It did not occur to me that a man would die when I pulled the trigger of that rifle.

I neither hated the man nor wanted him dead, but I feared him.

Johansen fired. I fired.

The figures disappeared in the flash of my muzzle. Johansen hollered at us to put our M-16's on automatic, and we sent hundreds of bullets out across the paddy. Someone threw a grenade out at them.

With daybreak, Captain Johansen and the artillery lieutenant walked over and found a man with a bullet hole in his head. There were no weapons. The dead man carried a pouch of papers, some rice, tobacco, canned fish, and he wore a blue-green uniform. That, at least, was Johansen's report. I would not look. I wondered what the other two men, the lucky two, had done after our volley. I wondered if they'd stopped to help the dead man, if they had been angry at his death, or only frightened that *they* might die. I wondered if the dead man were a relative of the others and, if so, what it must have been to leave him lying in the rice. I hoped the dead man was not named Li.

Later, Johansen and the lieutenant talked about the mechanics of the ambush. They agreed it had been perfectly executed. They were mildly upset that with such large and well-defined targets we had not done better than one in three. No matter. The platoons had registered other kills. They were talking these matters over, the officers pleased with their success and the rest of us relieved it was over, when my friend Chip and a squad leader named Tom were blown to pieces as they swept the village with the Third Platoon.

That was Alpha Company's most successful ambush.

X

The Man at the Well

He was just an old man, an old Vietnamese farmer. His hair was white, and he was somewhere over seventy years, stooped and hunched from work in the paddies, his spine bent into a permanent, calcified arc. He was blind. His eyes were huge and empty, glistening like aluminum under the sun, cauterized and burnt out. But the old man got around.

In March we came to his well. He stood and smiled while we used the water. He laughed when we laughed. To be ingratiating he said, "Good water for good GI's." Whenever there was occasion, he repeated the phrase.

Some children came to the well, and one of them, a little girl with black hair and hoops of steel through her ears, took the old fellow's hand, helping him about. The kids giggled at our naked bodies. A boy took a soldier's rifle from out of the mud and wiped it and stacked it against a tree, and the old man smiled.

Alpha Company decided to spend the day in the old man's village. We lounged inside his hut, and when resupply choppers brought down cold beer and food, we ate and wasted away the day. The kids administered professional back rubs, chopping and stretching and pushing our blood. They eyed our C rations, and the old blind man helped when he could.

When the wind stopped and the flies became bothersome, we went to the well again. We showered, and the old fellow helped, dipping into the well and yanking up buckets of water and sloshing it over our heads and backs and bellies. The kids watched him wash us. The day was as hot and peaceful as a day can be.

The blind old farmer was showering one of the men. A blustery and stupid soldier, blond hair and big belly, picked up a carton of milk and from fifteen feet away hurled it, for no reason, aiming at the old man and striking him flush in the face. The carton burst. Milk sprayed into the old man's cataracts. He hunched forward, rocking precariously and searching for balance. He dropped his bucket. His hands went to his eyes then dropped loosely to his thighs. His blind gaze fixed straight ahead, at the stupid soldier's feet. His tongue moved a little, trying to get at the cut and tasting the blood and milk. No one moved to help. The kids were quiet. The old man's eyes did a funny trick, almost rolling out of his head, out of sight. He was motionless, and finally he smiled. He picked up the bucket and with the ruins of goodness spread over him, perfect gore, he dunked into the well and came up with water, and he began showering the next soldier.

XI

Assault

On the twelfth day of April, Erik wrote me, and on the sixteenth day I sat on a rucksack and opened his letter. He was at Long Binh, working as a transportation clerk. I was on a hill. It was a hill in the middle of the bomb-grayed Batangan Peninsula, at a place we called Landing Zone Minuteman.

April 16 was hot, just as every day in April had been hot. First, in the April mornings, came the signs of the day. An absolutely cloudless sky crept out of the dark over the sea. The early mornings were clear, like a kind of distorted glass. A person could see impossible things. But the sun mounted, and the sky focused it on LZ Minuteman. By ten o'clock each morning, the rifles and uncovered canteens and ammo were untouchable. We let the stuff lay.

Sometimes, before the tepid swamp of air moved into its killer phase, Captain Johansen would move us off LZ Minuteman and we would sweat out the April morning on the march. We would search a hamlet carelessly, hurrying to get out of the sun. We would taunt some Vietnamese, applaud an occasional well or creek, find nothing, and finally retire to the top of our hill for the worst of each day.

We ignored the Viet Cong. We fought over piles of dead wood. We hacked poles out of the stuff, rammed them into the ground, and spread our ponchos over the poles, forming little roofs. Then we lay like prisoners in the resulting four square feet of shade.

The sun owned the afternoon. It broiled Alpha Company, that dusty red hill the skillet. We came to accept the sun as our most persistent and cunning enemy. All the training and discipline and soldierly skill in the world vanished during those April afternoons. We slept under our shelters, off guard, and no one cared. We waited for resupply. Occasionally a patrol would go down the hill to search out water. I sat with the radio, prodding and sometimes begging the rear to speed things up. Alpha was a fat company. We took our oranges and sacks of cold Coke for granted, like haircuts and bullets. There could be no war without them.

During those April afternoons Captain Johansen or the artillery officer would call for the chess set, and we passed time watching my white, clean army succumb. We wrote letters. We slept. I tried poetry and short stories. Other times we talked, and I tried to pry Johansen into conversation about the war. But he was an officer, and he was practical, and he would only talk tactics or history, and if I asked his opinion about the politics or morality of it all, he was ready with a joke or a shrug, sending the conversations into limbo or to more certain ground. Johansen was the best man around, and during the April afternoons it was sad he wore his bars.

The rest of the men talked about their girls, about R & R and where they would go and how much they would drink and where the girls performed the best tricks. I was a believer during those talks. The vets told it in a real, firsthand way that made you hunger for Thailand and Manila. When they said to watch for the ones with razor blades in their vaginas—communist agents—I believed, imagining the skill and commitment of those women.

We lay under our shelters and talked about rumors. On the sixteenth of April the rumor was that Alpha Company would be leaving soon. We would be CA'd into Pinkville. Men uttered the rumor carefully, trying to phrase it in more dramatic ways than it had come to them. But the words were drama enough. We feared Pinkville. We feared the Combat Assault. Johansen gave no hints, so we waited for resupply and hoped it wasn't so.

At three in the afternoon my radio buzzed and word came that resupply was inbound. Johansen had us spread out security for the chopper. When the pile of sacks and jugs and boxes was tossed off the bird, he hollered for everyone to stop clustering around the stuff. It was the big moment of April 16, and we were nothing but the children and hot civilians of the war, naked and thirsty and without pride. The stuff was dispersed. By three-thirty we had returned to our shelters, swearing that if the sun was our worst enemy, then the Coca-Cola Company certainly snuggled in as our best friend.

Next in order was the mail. And Erik:

Unclothed, poetry is much like newspaper writing, an event of the mind, the advent of an idea —bam!—you record it like a spring flood or the latest quintuplets. Which, after a sorely strained metaphor, brings me to the subject of the poems you sent me. If Frost was correct when he said a poem must be like a cake of ice on a stove, riding on its own melting, then the *Dharma* poem rides well indeed. I especially like the lines "truly/

brutally/we are the mercenaries of a green and wet forest"; also, the juxtaposition of the last line to the whole of the poem is so effortless, so ephemeral, like the last ice crystal made liquid, that I can't help but regret its melting: "Moksa, which is freedom."

In the rather limited reading I've done lately, I've discovered the poet Robinson Jeffers. His writing is harsh yet beautiful, and it makes me think of April, and April turns me to *The Waste Land,* and for a reason I do fully understand, the first lines of *The Waste Land* turn my thoughts not to England, but rather to you, here, in Vietnam. Take care. For it is not a fantasy:

> April is the cruelest month, breeding
> Lilacs out of the dead land, mixing
> Memory and desire, stirring
> Dull roots with spring rain.

April went on without lilacs. Without rain. When the choppers came in, they scooped dunes of red dust off LZ Minuteman, stirring the soil in their rotor blades, spewing clouds of rust color for a hundred yards. We learned to hide when the choppers made their drops. We stuffed our clean paper and clothes and apples into plastic bags. Minuteman was like the planet Mars. The place was desolate, hostile, utterly and vastly boring.

The days in April multiplied like twins, sextuplets, each identical. We played during the days. Volleyball. Gin. Tag. Poker or chess. Mad Mark had fun with his riot gas grenades, tossing them into a bunker and watching the artillery officer scramble out in tears. Captain Johansen and the battalion commander,

Colonel Daud, flew overhead in a helicopter, dumping gas grenades onto the LZ. It was a training exercise. The idea was to test our reaction time, to make sure our gas masks were functioning. Mostly, though, it was to pass away the month of April.

At night we were supposed to send out ambushes, orders of Colonel Daud. Sometimes we did, other times we did not. If the officers decided that the men were too tired or too restless for a night's ambush, they would prepare a set of grid coordinates and call them into battalion headquarters. It would be a false report, a fake. The artilleryman would radio phony information to the big guns in the rear. The 105's or 155's would blast out their expensive rounds of marking explosives, and the lieutenant would call back his bogus adjustments, chewing out someone in the rear for poor marksmanship. During the night's radio watch, we would call our nonexistent ambush, asking for a nonexistent situation report. We'd pause a moment, change our voice by a decibel, and answer our own call: "Sit Rep is negative. Out." We did this once an hour for the entire night, covering the possibility that higher headquarters might be monitoring the net. Foolproof. The enlisted men, all of us, were grateful to Alpha's officers. And the officers justified it, muttering that Colonel Daud was a greenhorn, too damn gung-ho. Phony ambushes were good for morale, best game we played on LZ Minuteman.

The rumors persisted. Near the end of the month they picked up steam; they became specific. Alpha Company would be CA'd into the My Lai area. A long operation. The helicopters would carry us to Pinkville before the end of the month. But the rumors had no source. To ask for a source was folly, for you would eventually be referred to the sun or to the rice or to a man who would have to ask someone else. Johansen only shrugged.

Four days before the end of the month, we were pulled off LZ Minuteman. We were given three days of rest in Chu Lai, a sprawling and safe military base along the South China Sea. Drinking, whistling, and gaping at the women in the floor shows, we killed the days and nights. On the final day of rest, Colonel Daud confirmed it. He played a strong but loving father. He drew Alpha Company into a semicircle and told everyone to be at ease.

"You're going after the VC Forty-eighth Battalion," he said. He was a black man, a stout and proper soldier. He didn't smile, but we were supposed to like him for that. "The Forty-eighth Battalion is a helluva fighting unit. They're tough. Some of you have tangled with them before. They're smart. That's what makes them tough. They'll hit you when you're sleeping. You look down to tie your boot laces, and they'll hit you. You fall asleep on guard—they'll massacre you. You walk along the trails, where they plant the mines because Americans are lazy and don't like to walk in the rice paddies, and they'll blow you all back to the world. Dead."

Colonel Daud seemed to think we were a bunch of morons. He thought he was teaching us, helping us to live. And he was sending us out there anyway.

"Okay. So you gotta be smart, too. You gotta be smarter. You're American soldiers. You're stronger than the dink. You're bigger. You're faster. You're better educated. You're better supplied, better trained, better supported. All you need is brains. Common sense will do it. If you're sleepy on guard, wake up a buddy, have him take over. Be alert while you're on the march. Watch the bushes. Keep an eye out for

109

freshly turned earth. If something seems out of place, stay clear of it and tell your buddy to stay clear. Okay? Pinkville is a bad place, I know that. But if you're dumb, you'll die in New York City."

Daud flew away in his helicopter. "Christ, what a pompous asshole." It was an officer. "Sends us to Pinkville and says we'll be okay if we're smart. New York, my ass."

I wrote a letter to Erik. Then there was a floor show. A Korean stripper started in her black evening gown and silver jewelry. She did it to Paul Simon and Arthur Garfunkel's music. *Homeward bound, I wish I was, homeward bound.* She had big breasts, big for a gook everyone said, damn sure. Pinkville. Christ, of all the places in the world, it would be Pinkville. The mines. Sullen, twisted dinks.

The Korean stripped suddenly, poked a tan and prime-lean thigh through a slit in the black gown. She was the prettiest woman in the Orient. Her beastly, unnaturally large breasts quivered like Jello.

The men cheered when the gown slid by wonderful accident from her shoulders.

It seemed to embarrass her, and she rolled her back, turning slightly away from Alpha Company and flexing her shoulderblades.

She was in time with the music. She unwrapped herself. She took up a baton, and she prodded herself with it.

The band played Beatles music, *Hey, Jude, don't be afraid. Take a sad song and make it better. Remember.* The girl finished stripping and sang the words. *And anytime you feel the pain, Hey Jude, refrain, don't carry the world upon your shoulder.*

Everyone sang, slowly and with an ache, getting

drunk, and the Korean beat time against her brown leg.

On April 29 we were on the helipad before dawn. With a hangover and with fear, it is difficult to put a helmet on your head. The helmet seems heavy and awkward. It is painful, in a slow and torturous way, to stumble to the pad under a sixty-pound rucksack, not easy to tote a rifle.

We lay in private groups on the tarred parking lot of an airfield. The black soldiers joked and were too loud for the early morning. They had their own piece of the helipad, and only officers would interrupt them. Out over the sea the sun began to light the day. Captain Johansen talked with his lieutenants; then he lay on his back. We smoked and thought about the Korean stripper and about hometowns. I made a communications check with battalion headquarters, wiped off my M-16, and put oil on the working parts. Some of the men complained about having to carry extra M-60 ammunition. The squad leaders were harsh, trying to be leaders in the morning. We exchanged cans of C rations, turkey loaf for pork slices, applesauce for peaches. All the noise ruined the early morning, the time when pure silence is only right, the time that is for thought alone.

With the first sunlight, Colonel Daud flew over. He radioed down. The first formation of choppers had an ETA of 0605 hours they would arrive in four minutes. The landing zone in Pinkville seemed quiet, he said. Fourteen miles to the south, the villagers of My Khe were sleeping.

Then the helicopters came in. They carried the day's hard light with them. It was already hot. Third Platoon and the command unit waddled to the bird and climbed in. We knelt or sat with our legs dangling over the open lips of the choppers. We shouted, trying to cheer up our friends. The helicopters roared, rose very slowly, dipped their noses forward, and climbed.

It was a short, hopelessly short ride. Chu Lai and the jets and PX's and clubs and libraries and USO and friendly beaches were down there; then came the guard towers and fences; and then came the countryside. Clusters of hamlets, paddies, hedgegrows, tunnel openings. Riding along, we watched for movement along the trails. It was too early.

You begin to sweat. Even with the rotor blades whipping cold air around like an air-conditioner, you sweat.

You light a cigarette, trying to think of something to say. A good joke would help, something funny. Laughing makes you believe you are resigned if not brave.

You stare at the faces. The Vietnamese scout, a kid who looked younger than my fourteen-year-old brother, was scared. Some of the other men seemed unconcerned. I felt tired, thinking I should be in bed, wondering if I were ill.

Johansen pointed down. It was an expanse of rice paddy, bordered on one side by a ridge of forest and on the other side by one of the villages of My Khe. "That's the place," he said. "When we begin the descent, grab my shoulder harness and hold on. If I'm hit, I don't want to fall out of this chopper."

We started to go down. The worst part of the Combat Assault, the thing you think about on the way down, is how perfectly exposed you are. Nowhere to hide. A fragile machine. No foxholes, no rocks, no gullies. The CA is the army's most potent offensive tactic of the war, a cousin to Hitler's blitzkrieg. The words are "agile," "hostile," and "mobile." One moment the world is serene, in another moment the war is there. It is like the cloudburst, like lightning, like the dropping of the bomb on a sleeping Hiroshima, like the Nazis' rush through Belgium and Poland and France.

You sit in your helicopter, watching the earth come spinning up at you. You jam your magazine into the rifle.

We came in at tree level, and the helicopter's machine guns opened up on the forested ridge, spraying down protective fire.

I held on to Johansen's shoulder straps. We waited for the crack of enemy fire, trying to hear above the sound of the bird and our own fire. The helicopter nestled into its landing area, hovering and trembling over the paddy, and we piled out like frantic rats. We scrambled for paddy dikes and depressions and rocks.

Bates lay beside me. "Jesus," he whispered, "I got a fire burning in my gut, I'm so scared. A big fire right in my gut."

There was no incoming fire, a cold LZ. Johansen waited until the helicopters were in the sky again. Running and waving, he got us to our feet, and we raced to search out the village. Someone spotted Vietnamese running from the village on the northern edge. We chased them. We felt confident and happy to be alive, and we felt brave. Simply surviving the assault was blessing enough, something of a mandate for aggressiveness, and we charged like storm troopers through My Khe.

It ended with two dead enemy soldiers and one dead American, a fellow I clobbered in Ping-Pong back in Chu Lai.

More Combat Assaults came in the next days. We learned to hate Colonel Daud and his force of heli-

113

copters. When he was killed by sappers in a midnight raid, we heard the news over the radio. A lieutenant led us in song, a catchy, happy, celebrating song: Ding-dong, the wicked witch is dead. We sang in good harmony. It sounded like a choir.

XII

Mori

She had been shot once. The bullet tore through her green uniform and into her buttock and out through her groin. She lay on her side, sprawled against a paddy dike. She never opened her eyes.

She moaned a little, not much, but she screamed when the medic touched at her wound. Blood gushed out of the holes, front and back.

Her face lay in dirt. Flies were all over her. There was no shade. It was mid-afternoon of a hot day. The medic said he did not dare squirt morphine into her, it would kill her before the wound did. He tried to patch the holes, but she squirmed and twisted, rocked and swayed, never opening her eyes. She flickered in and out of consciousness.

"She's a pretty woman, pretty for a gook. You don't see many pretty gooks, that's damn sure."

"Yes. Trouble is, she's shot dead through the wrong place." A dozen GI's hovered over her.

"Look at that blood come, Jesus. Like a fuckin' waterfall, like fuckin' Niagara Falls. She's gonna die quick. Can't mend up them bullet holes, no way."

"Fuckin'-aye. She's wasted."

"I wish I could help her." The man who shot her knelt down. "Didn't know she was a woman, she just looked like any dink. God, she must hurt. Get the damn flies off her, give her some peace."

She stretched her arms out above her head. She spread her fingers wide and put her hands into the dirt and squeezed in a sort of rhythm. Her forehead was wrinkled in a dozen long, flushed creases; her eyes were closed.

The man who shot her peered into her face. He asked if she couldn't be given shade.

"She's going to die," one soldier said.

"But can't we give her some shade?" He swatted at a cloud of flies over her head.

"Can't carry her, she won't let us. She's NVA, green uniform and everything. Hell, she's probably an NVA nurse, she probably *knows* she's just going to die. Look at her squeeze her hands. Trying to hurry and press all the blood out of herself."

We called for a dustoff helicopter and the company spread out in a wide perimeter around the shot woman. It was a long wait, partly because she was going to die, helicopter or no helicopter, and partly because she was with the enemy.

Her hair was lustrous black. The man who shot her stroked her hair. Two other soldiers and a medic stood beside her, fanning her and waving at the flies. Her uniform was crusted an almost black color from her blood, and the wound hadn't clotted much. The man who shot her held his canteen to her lips and she drank some Kool-Aid.

Then she twisted her head from side to side. She pulled her legs up to her chest and rocked, her whole body swaying. The man who shot her poured a trickle of water onto her forehead.

Soon she stopped swaying. She lay still and seemed either dead or unconscious. The medic felt her pulse and shrugged and said she was still going, just barely. She moaned now and then, almost talking in her sleep, but she was not being shrill or hysterical. The medic said she was not feeling any more pain.

"Damn, she is pretty. It's a crime. We could have shot an ugly old man instead."

When the helicopter came, she was still. Some soldiers lifted her onto a poncho and took her to the chopper. She lay curled up on the floor of the helicopter, then the bird roared and went into the air. Soon the pilot radioed down and asked what we were doing, making him risk his neck for sake of a dead woman.

XIII

My Lai in May

The villages of My Lai are scattered like wild seed in and around Pinkville, a flat stretch of sandy red clay along the northern coast of South Vietnam. "Pinkville" is a silly, county-fairish misnomer for such a sullen piece of the world. From the infantryman's perspective, zigzagging through one of the most heavily mined areas in the war zone, there is little pink or rosy about Pinkville: mud huts more often deserted than not, bombed-out pagodas, the patently hostile faces of Pinkville's inhabitants, acre after acre of slush, paddy after paddy, a dirty maze of elaborate tunnels and bomb shelters and graves.

The place gets its name from the fact that military maps color it a shimmering shade of elephant pink, signifying what the map legends call a "built-up area." Perhaps it once was. Perhaps Pinkville once upon a time was a thriving part of Quang Ngai province. It is no longer.

Pinkville and the villages called My Lai were well known to Alpha Company. Even before the headlines and before the names Calley and Medina took their place in history, Pinkville was a feared and special place on the earth. In January, a month or so before I arrived in Vietnam, less than a year after the slaughter in My Lai 4, Alpha Company took part in massive Operation Russell Beach, joining forces with other army elements, boatloads of marines, the navy and air force. Subject of the intricately planned and much-touted campaign was Pinkville and the Batangan Peninsula. Both had long served as Charlie's answer to the American R & R center—friendly natives, home-cooked rice, and nearly total sanctuary from American foot soldiers. Despite publicity and War College strategy, the operation did not produce the anticipated results, and this unit learned some hard lessons about Pinkville. There was no reliable criterion by which to distinguish a pretty Vietnamese girl from a deadly enemy; often they were one and the same person. The unit triggered one mine after another during Operation Russell Beach. Frustration and anger built with each explosion and betrayal, one Oriental face began to look like any other, hostile and black, and Alpha Company was boiling with hate when it was pulled out of Pinkville.

In May we were ordered back. Inserted by chopper in the villages of My Khe, a few thousand meters south of the My Lai's, we hit immediate contact. The Viet Cong were there, waiting in ambush across the paddy. The people of My Khe 3 were silent; they let us walk into the ambush, not a word of warning.

The day was quiet and hot, and I was thinking about Coke and rest. Then the bushes just erupted. I was carrying the radio for the company commander, and I remember getting separated from him, thinking I had to get up there. But I couldn't. I lay there. I screamed, buried my head.

A hand grenade came out of the bushes, skidded across my helmet, a red sardine can with explosives inside. I remember my glimpse of the thing, fizzling there beside me. I remember rolling to my left; remember waiting for the loudest noise of my life. It was just a pop, but I remember thinking that must be how it sounds to a dead man. Nothing hurt much. Clauson, a big fellow, took the force of the grenade. I lay there and watched him trot a few steps, screaming; then he lay on his back and screamed. I couldn't move. I kept hollering, begging for an end to it. The battalion commander was on the radio, asking where my captain was, wanting to talk to him, wanting me to pop smoke to mark our position, wanting me to call the other platoons. Bullets were coming from the bushes. Clauson was gone, I don't know where or how, and when I put my head up to look for him, I couldn't see anyone. Everything was noise, and it lasted on and on. It was over, I knew, when Mad Mark came out of the bushes, carrying a tall, skinny guy named Arnold over his shoulder. He swiveled Arnold into a helicopter, and we went north, into the My Lai's.

Along the way we encountered the citizens of Pinkville; they were the nonparticipants in war. Children under ten years, women, old folks who planted their eyes into the dirt and were silent. "Where are the VC?" Captain Johansen would ask, nicely enough. "Where are all the men? Where is Poppa-san?" No answers, not from the villagers. Not until we ducked poppa's bullet or stepped on his land mine.

Alpha Company was fatigued and angry leaving My Lai 5. Another futile search of a nearly deserted village, another fat zero turned up through interrogation. Moving north to cross the Diem Diem River, the company took continuous sniper fire, and it intensified into a sharp thunder when we reached the river and a bridge, seventy-five meters long and perfectly exposed, the only way across. One man at a time, churning as fast as the rucksacks and radios and machine guns al-

lowed, the unit crossed the Song Diem Diem, the rest
of the troops spraying out protective fire, waiting their
own turn, and we were scared. It was a race. A lieutenant was the starter, crouched at the clay runway leading into the paddy, hollering "Go" for each of us, then
letting loose a burst of fire to cover the guy. The captain, first man to win his race, was at the finish line.
He gave the V sign to each man across. It may have
signaled victory or valor. It did not mean peace. The
men were angry. No enemy soldiers to shoot back at,
only hedgerows and bushes and clumps of dead trees.

We were mortared that night. We crawled about in
gullies and along paddy dikes, trying to evade. We saw
the red quick flashes of their mortar tubes, but no one
dared fire back, for it would do nothing but give away
more precisely our position. The captain had me call
headquarters to get gunships, and in the middle of the
communication the mortar rounds fell even closer,
and Johansen muttered that they were bracketing us,
walking their rounds in from two directions, and on
our hands and knees, my antenna dragging along in
the paddy, the night purely black, we crawled forward and backward and finally into a village of My Lai,
where we spent that night. Platoons lay out in the
water of the paddies. They were afraid to move.

In the next days it took little provocation for us to
flick the flint of our Zippo lighters. Thatched roofs
take the flame quickly, and on bad days the hamlets of
Pinkville burned, taking our revenge in fire. It was
good to walk from Pinkville and to see fire behind
Alpha Company. It was good, just as pure hate is
good.

We walked to other villages, and the phantom
Forty-eighth Viet Cong Battalion walked with us.
When a booby-trapped artillery round blew two pop-

ular soldiers into a hedgerow, men put their fists into the faces of the nearest Vietnamese, two frightened women living in the guilty hamlet, and when the troops were through with them, they hacked off chunks of thick black hair. The men were crying, doing this. An officer used his pistol, hammering it against a prisoner's skull.

Scraps of our friends were dropped in plastic body bags. Jet fighters were called in. The hamlet was leveled, and napalm was used. I heard screams in the burning black rubble. I heard the enemy's AK-47 rifles crack out like impotent popguns against the jets. There were Viet Cong in that hamlet. And there were babies and children and people who just didn't give a damn in there, too. But Chip and Tom were on the way to Graves Registration in Chu Lai, and they were dead, and it was hard to be filled with pity.

We continued the march. The days baked red clay into our hides. One afternoon in mid-May we set up a defensive perimeter atop a high and safely steep hill, and we rested, taking a resupply of hot food, mail, Coke, and beer. Below us farmers worked in their paddies. A lieutenant—the one who earned the nickname Mad Mark—perched on a rock, pushed his spectacles against his nose, peered through the sniper scope mounted on his new M-14 rifle, and squeezed off a bullet at one of the farmers. The fellow fell. Mad Mark was elated: a bull's-eye at three hundred meters. When the lieutenant took a squad down to examine the results, he radioed back to me: "Wounded him in the leg. He's carrying rice and some papers in a small satchel. Call higher headquarters ASAP. Tell 'em we got one Victor Charlie, male, military-aged. Engaged with small-arms fire while trying to evade. How's your copy?"

I swallowed and said, "Good copy. Anything further?"

He paused. "Well, tell 'em the dink has a broken leg. Better get a dust-off out here. Save some chow for us."

Coming off the hill next day, a kid named Slocum hit a mine, shredding a leg. "Champion 48, this is Echo 40. Request urgent dust-off. Grid 788934. Urgent. I say again . . ."

And again that night. Small arms and grenades, two men wounded. Another man, lucky that time around, dislocated a shoulder as he dived for cover.

Following day, the officers decided to move us to the ocean. We took sniper fire along the way. My pack fell apart, rubber bands holding the radio antenna snapped, and the six-foot antenna dragged in the dirt. Mad Mark told me to wake up and get my shit together. But it was beginning not to matter. We walked like madmen, canteens going dry, and nothing stopped us. Finally came the sand, pines, a stretch of miraculously white beach, a sheaf of blue and perfect water—the South China Sea to the east of the My Lai's—and if we'd had a raft and courage, that ocean could have carried us a thousand miles and more toward home.

Instead, security was placed out in the pines, and we swam. We bellowed and grinned, weapons and ammo in the sand, not giving a damn. We slammed into the water. We punched at it and played in it, soaked our heads in it, slapped it to make cracking, smashing sounds, same as blasting a hand through glass.

Mail came. My girl friend traveled in Europe, with her boyfriend. My mother and father were afraid for me, praying; my sister was in school, and my brother

123

was playing basketball. The Viet Cong were nearby. They fired for ten seconds, and I got onto the radio, called for helicopters, popped smoke, and the medics carried three men to the choppers, and we went to another village.

XIV

Step Lightly

The Bouncing Betty is feared most. It is a common mine. It leaps out of its nest in the earth, and when it hits its apex, it explodes, reliable and deadly. If a fellow is lucky and if the mine is in an old emplacement, having been exposed to the rains, he may notice its three prongs jutting out of the clay. The prongs serve as the Bouncing Betty's firing device. Step on them, and the unlucky soldier will hear a muffled explosion; that's the initial charge sending the mine on its one-yard leap into the sky. The fellow takes another step and begins the next and his backside is bleeding and he's dead. We call it "ol' step and a half."

More destructive than the Bouncing Betty are the booby-trapped mortar and artillery rounds. They hang from trees. They nestle in shrubbery. They lie under the sand. They wait beneath the mud floors of huts. They haunted us. Chip, my black buddy from Orlando, strayed into a hedgerow and triggered a rigged 105 artillery round. He died in such a way that, for once, you could never know his color. He was wrapped in a plastic body bag, we popped smoke, and a helicopter took him away, my friend. And there was Shorty, a volatile fellow so convinced that the mines would take him that he spent a month AWOL. In July

125

he came back to the field, joking but still unsure of it all. One day, when it was very hot, he sat on a booby-trapped 155 round.

When you are ordered to march through areas such as Pinkville—GI slang for Song My, parent village of My Lai—the Batangan Peninsula or the Athletic Field, appropriately named for its flat acreage of grass and rice paddy, when you step about these pieces of ground, you do some thinking. You hallucinate. You look ahead a few paces and wonder what your legs will resemble if there is more to the earth in that spot than silicates and nitrogen. Will the pain be unbearable? Will you scream or fall silent? Will you be afraid to look at your own body, afraid of the sight of your own red flesh and white bone? You wonder if the medic remembered his morphine. You wonder if your friends will weep.

It is not easy to fight this sort of fear, but you try. You decide to be ultracareful—the hard-nosed, realistic approach. You try to second-guess the mine. Should you put your foot to that flat rock or the clump of weed to its rear? Paddy dike or water? You wish you were Tarzan, able to swing with the vines. You try to trace the footprints of the man to your front. You give it up when he curses you for following too closely; better one man dead than two.

The moment-to-moment, step-by-step decision-making preys on your mind. The effect sometimes is paralysis. You are slow to rise from rest breaks. You walk like a wooden man, like a toy soldier out of Victor Herbert's *Babes in Toyland*. Contrary to military and parental training, you walk with your eyes pinned to the dirt, spine arched, and you are shivering, shoulders hunched. If you are not overwhelmed by complete catatonia, you may react as Philip did on

126

the day he was told to police up one of his friends, victim of an antipersonnel mine. Afterward, as dusk fell, Philip was swinging his entrenching tool like a madman, sweating and crying and hollering. He dug a foxhole four feet into the clay. He sat in it and sobbed. Everyone—all his friends and all the officers—were very quiet, and not a person said anything. No one comforted him until it was very dark. Then, to stop the noise, one man at a time would talk to him, each of us saying he understood and that tomorrow it would all be over. The captain said he would get Philip to the rear, find him a job driving a truck or painting fences.

Once in a great while we would talk seriously about the mines. "It's more than the fear of death that chews on your mind," one soldier, nineteen years old, eight months in the field, said. "It's an absurd combination of certainty and uncertainty: the certainty that you're walking in mine fields, walking past the things day after day; the uncertainty of your every movement, of which way to shift your weight, of where to sit down.

"There are so many ways the VC can do it. So many configurations, so many types of camouflage to hide them. I'm ready to go home."

The kid is right:

The M-14 antipersonnel mine, nicknamed the "toe popper." It will take a hunk out of your foot. Smitty lost a set of toes. Another man who is now just a blur of gray eyes and brown hair—he was with us for only a week—lost his left heel.

The booby-trapped grenade. Picture a bushy shrub along your path of march. Picture a tin can secured to the shrub, open and directed toward the trail. Inside the can is a hand grenade, safety pin removed, so that only the can's metal circumference prevents the

127

"spoon," or firing handle, from jumping off the grenade and detonating it. Finally, a trip wire is attached to the grenade, extending across the pathway, perhaps six inches above the dirt. Hence, when your delicate size-eight foot caresses that wire, the grenade is yanked from its container, releasing the spoon and creating problems for you and your future.

The Soviet TMB and the Chinese antitank mines. Although designed to detonate under the pressure of heavy vehicles, the antitank mine is known to have shredded more than one soldier.

The directional-fragmentation mine. The concave-faced directional mine contains from 450 to 800 steel fragments embedded in a matrix and backed by an explosive charge—TNT or petnam. The mine is aimed at your anticipated route of march. Your counterpart in uniform, a gentle young man, crouches in the jungle, just off the trail. When you are in range, he squeezes his electronic firing device. The effects of the the mine are similar to those of a twelve-gauge shotgun fired at close range. United States Army training manuals describe this country's equivalent device, the Claymore mine: "It will allow for wider distribution and use, particularly in large cities. It will effect considerable savings in materials and logistics." In addition, they call the mine cold-blooded.

The corrosive-action-car-killer. The CACK is nothing more than a grenade, its safety pin extracted and spoon held in place by a rubber band. It is deposited in your gas tank. The corrosive action of the gasoline eats away the rubber band, releasing the spoon, blowing you up in a week or less. Although rarely encountered by the foot-borne infantryman, the device gives the rear-echelon mine finder (REMF) something to ponder as he delivers the general's laundry.

In the three days I spent writing this, mines and men came together three more times. Seven more legs, one more arm.

The immediacy of the last explosion—three legs, ten minutes ago—made me ready to burn the midsection of this report, the flippant itemization of these killer devices. Hearing over the radio what I just did, only enough for a flashing memory of what it is all about, makes the *Catch-22* jokes into a cemetery of half-truths. "Orphan 22, this is . . . this is Yankee 22 . . . mine, mine. Two guys . . . legs are off . . . I say again, legs off . . . request urgent dust-off grid 711888 . . . give me ETA . . . get that damn bird." Tactical Operations Center: "You're coming in distorted . . . Yankee 22? Say again . . . speak slowly . . . understand you need dust-off helicopter?" Pause. "This is Yankee 22 . . . for Chri . . . ake . . . need chopper . . . two men, legs are . . ."

But only to say another truth will I let the half-truths stand. The catalog of mines will be retained, because that is how we talked about them, with a funny laugh, flippantly, with a chuckle. It is funny. It's absurd.

Patent absurdity. The troops are going home, and the war has not been won, even with a quarter of the United States Army fighting it. We slay one of them, hit a mine, kill another, hit another mine. It is funny. We walk through the mines, trying to catch the Viet Cong Forty-eighth Battalion like inexperienced hunters after a hummingbird. But Charlie finds us far more often than we find him. He is hidden among the mass of civilians, or in tunnels, or in jungles. So we walk to find him, stalking the mythical, phantomlike Forty-eighth Battalion from here to there to here to there. And each piece of ground left behind is his from the

129

moment we are gone on our next hunt. It is not a war fought for territory, nor for pieces of land that will be won and held. It is not a war fought to win the hearts of the Vietnamese nationals, not in the wake of contempt drawn on our faces and on theirs, not in the wake of a burning village, a trampled rice paddy, a battered detainee. If land is not won and if hearts are at best left indifferent; if the only obvious criterion of military success is body count and if the enemy absorbs losses as he has, still able to lure us amid his crop of mines; if soldiers are being withdrawn, with more to go later and later and later; if legs make me more of a man, and they surely do, my soul and character and capacity to love notwithstanding; if any of this is truth, a soldier can only do his walking, laughing along the way and taking a funny, crooked step.

After the war, he can begin to be bitter. Those who point at and degrade his bitterness, those who declare that it's all a part of war and that this is a job which must be done—to those patriots I will recommend a postwar vacation to this land, where they can swim in the sea, lounge under a fine sun, stroll in the quaint countryside, wife and son in hand. Certainly, there will be a mine or two still in the earth. Alpha Company did not detonate all of them.

130

XV

Centurion

Alpha Company was resting in a village, using water from a deep well, when one of the men found an NVA rifle. It was hidden under a shrub. "Jesus, looky-looky! A little toy!" The man danced up and down, delighted. It was an AK-47, beat-up looking. A single banana shaped magazine of ammunition was wrapped in cloth beside the weapon. "And we thought this village was so nice and cozy! Ha, the sneaky bastards!"

Captain Johansen ordered us to search the rest of the village, and we searched until sundown, not finding a thing. The villagers watched sullenly. We tore up the floors of their huts and overturned huge jugs of rice an kicked straw out of pig styes. We poured sand into the well.

At dusk, the captain and his lieutenants conferred, finally deciding to take some prisoners for the night. "Where there's an AK-47, there's Charlie," the captain said. "Chances are he's here right now, living in the ville. And chances are he's got friends."

The lieutenants went into a hut and pulled out three old men. It was just at dusk, the sun gone. The lieutenants wrapped rope around the prisoners' wrists, then tied more rope around their ankles. They stood the three old men against three saplings and tied the men fast to the trees. "Better gag them," one of the

131

lieutenants said. So they stuffed wet rags into their mouths. When all this was done, it was night.

"Okay, that's good," the captain said. "Charlie won't attack tonight. We've got Poppa-san."

The night was clear. We ate C rations and drank some beer. Then the guard started, the ritual come alive from our pagan past—Thucydides and Polybius and Julius Caesar, tales of encampment, tales of night terror—the long silent stare into an opaque shell of shadows and dark. Three men to a foxhole: two asleep and one awake. No smoking: the enemy will see the light and blow your lungs out. Stay alert: courts-martial for those dozing on guard. All the rules passed down from ancient warfare, the lessons of dead men.

Twice that night I was on radio-watch, once at midnight and again near morning. I sat by the radio and watched the three men strapped to their saplings. They sagged, trying to sleep. One of them, the oldest, was completely limp, bending the little tree sharply to the ground, supported against it by a rope around his belly and another around his wrists. He looked like pictures of Ho Chi Minh. A fine pointed beard, a long face, wide and broadly-set eyes covered with drooping lids.

Bates, one of my good friends in the company, came over to sit with me. "It's appalling, isn't it? Making these old duffers dangle there all night."

"At least no one beat on them," I said. "I sort of expected it when the Kid found the AK-47."

"Still, what good will it do?" Bates said. "The old guys aren't going to talk. They talk to us, tell us where the rifle came from, and ol' Charlie will get to them. They don't talk and our interrogation teams rough them up. Wait till tomorrow, that's what will happen. I'd like to cut them loose. Right now."

"Maybe nothing will happen. If we aren't hit to-night, maybe we'll just let the old men go free."

Bates grunted. "This is war, my friend. You don't find a weapon and just walk away."

He went to sleep, leaving me with the radio and the three old men. They were only a few feet away, hanging to their saplings like the men at Golgotha. I went to the oldest of them and pulled his gag out and let him drink from my canteen. He didn't look at me. When he was through with his drinking, he opened his mouth wide for me and I tucked the rag inside. Then he opened his eyes and nodded and I patted him on the shoulder. The other two were sleeping, and I let them sleep.

In the morning one of the lieutenants beat on the old men. Alpha's Vietnamese scout shouted at them, whipping them in the legs with a long stick, whipping them across their thin, bony shins, screaming at them, trying to get them to say where the rifle came from, whipping the old men and making long cuts into their ankles. One of the old men, not the oldest, whimpered; none of them talked.

Then we released them and went on our way.

XVI

Wise Endurance

Captain Johansen watched the soldiers raise their bottles of beer to their mouths, drinking to the end of the day, another sunrise and finally another red line at the edge of the sky where the sun was disappearing. Johansen was separated from his soldiers by a deadfall canyon of character and temperament. They were there and he was here. He was quite alone, resting against his poncho and pack, his face at rest, his eyes relaxed against the coming of dark. He had no companions. He was about a week away from leaving command of Alpha Company, and a fine eight-hour job was ready for him in the rear.

Captain Johansen had watched the men for an hour. They had dug foxholes, shallow slices out of the hard clay; then they'd squirted mosquito repellent over themselves, spread their sleeping gear near their holes, and now they were drinking beer. The soldiers were happy. No enemy, no blood for over a week, nothing but night, then day.

"I'd rather be brave," he suddenly said to me. "I'd rather be brave than almost anything. How does that strike you?"

"It's nothing to laugh at, sir."

"What about yourself?"

"Sometimes I look back at those days around My

Lai, sir, and I wish I would have acted better, more bravely. I did my best, though. But I'll think about it."

A month before, on a blistering day, Johansen had charged a Viet Cong soldier. He'd killed him at chest-to-chest range, more or less, first throwing a grenade, then running flat out across a paddy, up to the Viet Cong's ditch, then shooting him to death. With the steady, blood-headed intensity of Sir Lancelot, Captain Johansen was brave. It was strange that he thought about it at all.

But I thought about it. Arizona, the dead kid I always remember first, died on the same day that Johansen's Viet Cong died. Arizona bulled out across a flat piece of land, just like the captain, and I only remember his long limp body in the grass. It's the charge, the light brigade with only one man, that is the first thing to think about when thinking about courage. People who do it are remembered as brave, win or lose. They are heroes forever. It seems like courage, the charge.

When I was a kid in eighth grade and not at all concerned about being brave except as a way to seem to other people, usually a pretty girl, I was pushed out of line while we were waiting for the school bus. The kid who did it was big. He had a flat-top haircut and freckles and a grin that meant he could massacre me if it came to that. Being big with words, I told him to go piss on the principal's desk, and he started shoving, the stiff-finger-on-the-chest technique, backing me up with little spurts of the wrist. Honor was clearly at stake. I was in the right and he was the kind of human being I detest most, a perfect bully. So I shoved back, and there was a little scuffle, then the bus came. Before I got off—rather, just as I was stepping out in front of my house—he hollered out for everyone to hear that there would be a fight the next Monday. It was Friday. I had three nights to ponder the prospect. There was no doubt about the outcome. There wasn't a chance. On Monday I went to the bus, being inconspicuous but not too inconspicuous; getting beat was a trifle better than hiding. I hoped he'd forgotten. Finally he fought me, and we danced around on the ice in front of the bicycle rack. I bobbed like hell, and the enemy fell twice, not that I ever hit him, and by all accounts it ended in a draw.

But at a place east of My Lai, within smell of the South China Sea, bullets seemed aimed straight at you.

Isolated, a stretch of meadow, the sound going into the air, through the air, right at your head, you writhe like a man suddenly waking in the middle of a heart transplant, the old heart out, the new one poised somewhere unseen in the enemy's hands. The pain, even with the ether or sodium chloride, explodes in the empty cavity, and the terror is in waiting for the cavity to be filled, for life to start pumping and throbbing again.

You whimper, low or screeching, and it doesn't start anywhere. The throat does the pleading for you, taking the heart's place, the soul gone. Numbness. Dumbness. No thoughts.

I was not at My Lai when the massacre occurred. I was in the paddies and sleeping in the clay, with Johansen and Arizona and Alpha Company, a year and more later. But if a man can squirm in a meadow, he can shoot children. Neither are examples of courage.

"You're a sensitive guy," Johansen said. "Go get me a beer from one of those soldiers, will you?" I fetched a beer and sat with the captain. "You don't have to carry the radio for me, you know. It's a good shot, the

136

antenna sticking up. You've done a good job, don't get me wrong, I knew you'd do a good job first time I saw you. But it's easy to get shot walking with me. Officers are favorite targets. The radio antenna's a good target, you know. VC knows damn well there's an officer around, so they shoot at it. And . . . well, you're a sensitive guy, like I said. Some guys are just numb to death."

"I'd just as soon go on," I said.

Johansen told me not to forget to call situation reports back to headquarters. He went off and checked the positions.

Courage is nothing to laugh at, not if it is proper courage and exercised by men who know what they do is proper. Proper courage is wise courage. It's acting wisely, acting wisely when fear would have a man act otherwise. It is the endurance of the soul in spite of fear—wisely. Plato, I recalled, wrote something like that. In the dialogue called *Laches*:

> SOCRATES: And now, Laches, do you try and tell me in like manner, What is that common quality which is called courage, and which includes all the various uses of the term when applied both to pleasure and pain, and in all the cases to which I was just referring?
>
> LACHES: I should say that courage is a sort of endurance of the soul, if I am to speak of the universal nature which pervades them all.
>
> SOCRATES: But that is what we must do if we are to answer our own question. And yet I cannot say that every kind of endurance is, in my opinion, to be deemed courage. Hear my reason. I am sure, Laches, that you would consider courage to be a very noble quality.

LACHES: Most noble, certainly.

SOCRATES: And you would say that a wise endurance is also good and noble?

LACHES: Very noble.

SOCRATES: But what would you say of a foolish
endurance? Is not that, on the other hand, to
be regarded as evil and hurtful?

LACHES: True. . . .

SOCRATES: Then, according to you, only the wise
endurance is courage?

LACHES: It seems so.

What, then, under the dispassionate moon of Vietnam, in the birdless, insectless silence—what, then, is
wise endurance? Despising bullyism as I did, thinking
the war wrong from the beginning—even in tenth
grade, writing a term paper on a war I never believed
I would have to fight—I had endured. I'd stayed on
through basic training, watching the fat kid named
Kline shivering in fear, thrusting my blade into the
rubber tires at the bayonet range, scoring expert with
the M-16. I'd endured through advanced infantry
training, with the rest of the draftees. I'd planned to
run away, to slip across the border in the dead of
night. I'd planned for two months, drawing maps and
researching at the Fort Lewis library, learning all the
terrible details about plane fares to Sweden, muffling
my voice over the telephone, making a lie to my parents to get them to send my passport and health
record. I'd almost not endured.

But was the endurance, the final midnight walk
over the tarred runway at Fort Lewis and up into the
plane, was it wise? There is the phrase: courage of conviction. Doubtless, I thought, conviction can be right
or wrong. But I had reasons to oppose the war in Viet-

138

nam. The reasons could be murmured like the Psalms on a cold-moon Vietnam night: Kill and fight only for certain causes; certain causes somehow involve self-evident truths; Hitler's blitzkrieg, the attack on Pearl Harbor, these were somehow self-evident grounds for using force, just as bullyism will, in the end, call for force; but the war in Vietnam drifted in and out of human lives, taking them or sparing them like a headless, berserk taxi hack, without evident cause, a war fought for uncertain reasons.

The conviction seemed right. And, if right, was my apparent courage in enduring merely a well-disguised cowardice? When my father wrote that at least his son was discovering how much he could take and still go on, was he ignoring his son's failure to utter a dramatic and certain and courageous no to the war? Was his son a fool? A sheep being stripped of wool that is his by right?

One day Alpha Company was strung out in a long line, walking from one village near Pinkville to another. Some boys were herding cows in a free-fire zone. They were not supposed to be there: legal targets for our machine guns and M-16's. We fired at them, cows and boys together, the whole company, or nearly all of it, like target practice at Fort Lewis. The boys escaped, but one cow stood its ground. Bullets struck its flanks, exploding globs of flesh, boring into its belly. The cow stood parallel to the soldiers, a wonderful profile. It looked away, in a single direction, and it did not move. I did not shoot, but I did endure, without protest, except to ask the man in front of me why he was shooting and smiling.

Alpha Company had a bad time near the My Lai's. Mines were the worst, every size and kind of mine. Toepoppers, Bouncing Betties, booby-trapped artillery and mortar rounds and hand grenades. Slocum, Smith, Easton, Dunn, Chip, Tom—all those soldiers walked on and on and on, enduring the terror, waiting, and the mines finally got them. Were they wise to keep walking? The alternative, looking back and listening to the radio and seeing Captain Johansen finish his rounds and return to his poncho, the alternative, I thought, was to sit on a single splotch of earth and silently wait for the war to end.

"Will you be glad to get to the rear, sir?"

"Sure," he said, grinning and with a shrug. "I'll miss the company. But I don't suppose I'll miss the war much."

"I don't know how you can be so dispassionate. God, I'd be hiding in my foxhole, a mile into the ground, just waiting for a chopper to take me out of here."

Captain Johansen rolled up in a poncho; he lay on his side and seemed to go to sleep.

Whatever it is, soldiering in a war is something that makes a fellow think about courage, makes a man wonder what it is and if he has it. Some say Ernest Hemingway was obsessed by the need to show bravery in battle. It started, they say, somewhere in World War I and ended when he passed his final test in Idaho. If the man was obsessed with the notion of courage, that was a fault. But, reading Hemingway's war journalism and his war stories, you get the sense that he was simply *concerned* about bravery, hence about cowardice, and that seems a virtue, a sublime and profound concern that few men have. For courage, according to Plato, is one of the four parts of virtue. It is there with temperance, justice, and wisdom, and all parts are necessary to make the sublime human being. In fact, Plato says, men without courage are men without temperance, justice, or wisdom, just as without wisdom men are not truly courageous. Men must *know* what they do is courageous, they must *know* it is right, and that kind of knowledge is wisdom and nothing else. Which is why I know few brave men. Either they are stupid and do not know what is right. Or they know what is right and cannot bring themselves to do it. Or they know what is right and do it, but do not feel and understand the fear that must be overcome. It takes a special man.

Courage is more than the charge.

More than dying or suffering the loss of a love in silence or being gallant.

It is temperament and, more, wisdom. Was the cow, standing immobile and passive, more courageous than the Vietnamese boys who ran like rabbits from Alpha Company's barrage? Hardly. Cows are very stupid.

Most soldiers in Alpha Company did not think about human courage. There were malingerers in Alpha Company. Men who cared little about bravery. "Shit, man, the trick of being in the Nam is gettin' *out* of the Nam. And I don't mean gettin' out in a plastic body bag. I mean gettin' out alive, so my girl can grab me so I'll know it." The malingerers manufactured some of the best, most persuasive ailments ever, some good enough to fool a skeptical high school nurse.

When we walked through the sultry villes and sluggish, sullen land called Pinkville, the mass of men in Alpha Company talked little about dying. To talk about it was bad luck, the ultimate self-fulfilling prophecy. Death was taboo. The word for getting killed was "wasted." When you hit a Bouncing Betty and it blows you to bits, you get wasted. Fear was taboo. It could be mentioned, of course, but it had to be accompanied with a shrug and a grin and obvious resignation. All this took the meaning out of courage. We could not gaze straight at fear and dying, not, at least, while out in the field, and so there was no way to face the question.

"You don't talk about being a hero, with a star pinned on your shirt and feeling all puffed up." The soldier couldn't understand when I asked him about the day he ran from his foxhole, through enemy fire, to wrap useless cloth around a dying soldier's chest. "I reacted, I guess. I just did it."

"Did it seem the right thing to do?"

"No," Doc said. "Not right, not wrong either."

"Did you think you might be shot?"

"Yes. I guess I did. Maybe not. When someone hollers for the medic, if you're a medic you run toward the shout. That's it, I guess."

"But isn't there the feeling you might *die*?"

Doc had his legs crossed and was leaning over a can of C rations. He seemed intent on them. "No. I won't die over here." He laughed. "Maybe I'll never die. I just wondered why I didn't feel anything hit me. Something should have hit me, there was so much firing. I sort of ran over, waiting for a kind of blast or punch in the back. My back always feels most exposed."

Before the war, my favorite heroes had been make-believe men. Alan Ladd of *Shane*, Captain Vere, Humphrey Bogart as the proprietor of Café d'Americain, Frederic Henry. Especially Frederic Henry. Henry was able to leave war, being good and brave enough at it, for real love, and although he missed the men of war, he did not miss the fear and killing. And Henry, like all my heroes, was not obsessed by courage; he

142

knew it was only one part of virtue, that love and justice were other parts.

To a man, my heroes before going to Vietnam were hard and realistic. To a man, they were removed from other men, able to climb above and gaze down at other men. Bogie in his office, looking down at roulette wheels and travelers. Vere, elevated; the *Star*, searching justice. Shane, loving the boy, detesting violence, looking down and saying good bye aboard that stocky horse.

To a man, my heroes were wise. Perhaps Vere was an exception. But when he allowed Billy Budd to die, he was at least seeking justice, tormented by a need for wisdom, even omniscience. But certainly Shane and Bogart and Henry had learned much and knew much, having gone through their special agonies.

And each was courageous. Bogie. How could a man leave Ingrid Bergman, send her away, even for the most noble of causes? Shane, facing his villain. Vere, sending a stuttering, blond, purely innocent youth to the gallows. And especially Frederic Henry. Talking with his love, Catherine Barkley:

> "You're brave."
> "No," she said. "But I would like to be."
> "I'm not," I said. "I know where I stand. I've been out long enough to know. I'm like a ball-player that bats two hundred and thirty and knows he's no better."
> "What is a ball-player that bats two hundred and thirty? It's awfully impressive."
> "It's not. It means a mediocre hitter in base-ball."
> "But still a hitter," she prodded me.

"I guess we're both conceited," I said. "But you are brave."

Henry, and the rest of my heroes, had been out long enough to know; experienced and wise. Batting two hundred and thirty? Realistic, able to speak the truth. Conceited? Never. And, most strikingly, each of the heroes *thought* about courage, *cared* about being brave, at least enough to talk about it and wonder to others about it.

But in Vietnam, out in the villages of My Lai and My Khe, where the question of courage is critical, no one except Captain Johansen seemed to care. Not the malingerers, certainly. Not Arizona, the kid who was shot in the chest in his private charge. Not the Doc. So, when the time in my life came to replace fictional heroes with real ones, the candidates were sparse, and it was to be the captain or no one.

Looking at him, only a shadow rolled in a poncho, lying on his side asleep, I wondered what it was about him that made him a real hero.

He was blond. Heroes somehow are blond in the ideal. He had driven racing automobiles as a civilian and had a red slab of scarred flesh as his prize. He had medals. One was for killing the Viet Cong, a Silver Star. He was like Vere, Bogie, Shane, and Frederic Henry, companionless among herds of other men, men lesser than he, but still sad and haunted that he was not perfect. At least, so it appeared. Perhaps other men, some of the troopers he led who were not so brave, died when he did not and should have, by a hero's standard.

Like my fictional prewar heroes, Captain Johansen's courage was a model. And just as I could never match Alan Ladd's prowess, nor Captain Vere's intensity of conviction, nor Robert Jordan's resolution to confront his own certain death (in Jordan's place, I would have climbed back on my horse, bad leg and all, and galloped away till I bled to death in the saddle), I could not match my captain. Still, I found a living hero, and it was good to learn that human beings sometimes embody valor, that they do not always dissolve at the end of a book or movie reel.

I thought about courage off and on for the rest of my tour in Vietnam. When I compared subsequent company commanders to Johansen, it was clear that he alone cared enough about being brave to think about it and try to do it. Captain Smith admitted that he was a coward, using just that word. Captain Forsythe strutted and pretended, but he failed.

On the outside, things did not change much after Captain Johansen. We lost about the same number of men. We fought about the same number of battles, always small little skirmishes.

But losing him was like the Trojans losing Hector. He gave some amount of reason to fight. Certainly there were never any political reasons. The war, like Hector's own war, was silly and stupid. Troy was besieged for the sake of a pretty woman. And Helen, for God's sake, was a woman most of the grubby, warted Trojans could never have. Vietnam was under siege in pursuit of a pretty, tantalizing, promiscuous, particularly American brand of government and style. And most of Alpha Company would have preferred a likable whore to self-determination. So Captain Johansen helped to mitigate and melt the silliness, showing the grace and poise a man can have under the worst of circumstances, a wrong war. We clung to him.

Even forgetting the captain, looking at myself and the days I writhed insensible under bullets and the

145

other days when I did okay, somehow shooting back or talking coherently into the radio or simply watching without embarrassment how the fighting went, some of the futility and stupidity disappeared. The idea is manliness, crudely idealized. You liken dead friends to the pure vision of the eternal dead soldier. You liken living friends to the mass of dusty troops who have swarmed the world forever. And you try to find a hero.

It is more difficult, however, to think of yourself in those ways. As the eternal Hector, dying gallantly. It is impossible. That's the problem. Knowing yourself, you can't make it real for yourself. It's sad when you learn you're not much of a hero.

Grace under pressure, Hemingway would say. That is how you recognize a brave man. But somehow grace under pressure is insufficient. It's too easy to affect grace, and it's too hard to see through it. I remembered the taut-faced GI's who gracefully buckled, copping out so smoothly, with such poise, that no one ever knew. The malingerers were adept: "I know we're in a tight spot, sir. I wouldn't go back to the rear, you know me. But—" then a straight-faced, solid, eye-to-eye lie. Grace under pressure means you can confront things gracefully or squeeze out of them gracefully. But to make those two things equal with the easy word "grace" is wrong. Grace under pressure is not courage.

Or the other cliché: A coward dies a thousand deaths but a brave man only once. That seems wrong, too. Is a man once and for always a coward? Once and for always a hero?

It is more likely that men act cowardly and, at other times, act with courage, each in different measure, each with varying consistency. The men who do well on the average, perhaps with one moment of glory, those men are brave.

And those who are neither cowards nor heroes, those men sweating beads of pearly fear, failing and whimpering and trying again—the mass of men in Alpha Company—even they may be redeemable. The easy aphorisms hold no hope for the middle man, the man who wants to try but has already died more than once, squirming under the bullets, going through the act of death and coming through embarrassingly alive. The bullets stop. As in slow motion, physical things gleam. Noise dissolves. You tentatively peek up, wondering if it is the end. Then you look at the other men, reading your own caved-in belly deep in their eyes. The fright dies the same way novocaine wears off in the dentist's chair. You promise, almost moving your lips, to do better next time; that by itself is a kind of courage.

XVII

July

Captain Johansen was one of the nation's pride. He was blond, meticulously fair, brave, tall, blue-eyed, and an officer. He left Alpha Company at the end of June.

Standing bareheaded up on a little hill, Johansen said we were a good outfit, he was proud of us, he was sad some of the men were dead or crippled. There was a brief change-of-command ceremony. We all stood at attention, feeling like orphans up for adoption. We watched Johansen salute and shake hands with our new commander, a short, fat ROTC officer.

The new captain looked like a grown-up Spanky of "Our Gang."

Like seventy percent of the officers around, he was from the South, a Tennessean named Smith. He planted his legs and gave us a pep talk. He wanted a good, tough fighting unit. He wanted professionals, he said, just as the battalion motto called for in big gold letters. He tried to sound authoritative, but it did not work. No one trusts a green officer, and if he's short and fat and thinks he's a good soldier, he had better be Patton himself.

With Smith leading Alpha Company, we returned to the My Lai–My Khe area. It was a two-day operation, simply a sweep through a string of villages; we would make camp for the night, then sweep right back again the next day.

A troop of tracks—armored personel carriers, tank-like vehicles but without the cannon—accompanied us.

Helicopters ferried us into a paddy to the north of one of the villages at My Khe. Smith's face was red. He yelled at everyone, and nobody listened. He told us to spread out, watch the tree line.

"Damn it, Timmy boy, we're gonna get killed here. Those guys better spread out. Jesus, they act like they been smokin' a weed we grow back home."

Then he smiled like a jolly fat man and said he always wanted to be a soldier. "My daddy used to say, Bobby, stay away from women and hard liquor. Join the army, my daddy said. Join the army and stay with it, and you'll live to be a hundred. But, by cracker, those guys better keep their eyes open. Intel says this place is bad."

We waited for the tracks. When they came, the second platoon took the lead through the village while the heavy stuff lumbered up a hill to give us cover with their fifty-caliber machine guns. The idea was to drive the enemy from the hamlet and into the open, where the tracks could gun them down.

The first hamlets were deserted. We went slowly. One of the men on point cleared a trail with a mine detector. But he'd never used one before, and no one believed the thing worked anyway. With twenty years' shrapnel in the ground, the headphones are always clicking, mines or no mines. We poked around a little, trying not to touch anything, but you don't find the Viet Cong that way. We just walked. That was the order, the plan, and we tried to do it silently and safely. The third hamlet was full of women and children. We herded them out into an adjacent paddy, and the

149

tracks came off their hill, and we smoked and handed out C rations while Captain Smith and the track commander argued about what to do next. They decided to take the civilians along to our night position, and the logic was clear. Their husbands and fathers were the people we were looking for. We'd be safe with the women and kids sleeping with us. So we hauled up the old women, and the kids climbed aboard, and we churned out into the middle of a putrid, wet rice paddy. The tracks formed a circle. In silence, the civilians huddled in the middle of the perimeter, as if they'd done it before, and they went to sleep.

Captain Smith sat by the radio. "Pretty good strategy, huh, Timmy boy? ROTC's pretty good trainin', not so bad as they say. Hee, hee. Actually, to tell the truth now, it is pretty bad trainin'. Should've gone to the Point, I guess, but oh well, Daddy always said, start at the bottom. Hee, hee. An' ROTC's the bottom." He paused a moment and changed his tone, going into the authoritative one. "Call headquarters. Tell 'em we got our night position. No ambushes. Code it up and tell 'em we're moving out early tomorrow."

We moved out at daybreak, leaving the civilians behind. Smith ordered us to check out bunkers and bomb shelters as we swept back through the villages. One of the grenades brought an old lady out of her bomb shelter. She was seventy years old and bleeding all over. The medics patched her as best they could. She was conscious. She watched them wrap bandages around her breasts. They jabbed her with morphine. Then we called a dust-off helicopter, and when it arrived the medics tried to help her up. She scrambled like a wet fish. She was nearly dead, but she crawled away on all fours, whimpering, trying to get back into her hole. The medics had to carry her. She hollered all the way. The bandages were dangling, blood was in her hair and eyes, she was screaming, but the bird roared and lifted and dipped its nose and flew away with her.

That was the end of the mission.

We climbed onto the tracks, hung our packs on hooks, removed our helmets, and dangled our legs over the sides. I felt good. I tied the radio to the side of the track and lay on my back to talk with the other platoons. We turned out of the villages and into the rice paddy. It was a marsh. The mud was up to a man's thigh.

Rocket-propelled grenades came out of the village. They hit in front of the lead vehicles.

"Incoming! Jesus, get the hell off these tracks!" The fifty-caliber gunner was hollering at us. "Get off here, let me shoot!"

Small-arms fire came next, spraying the water.

We dived off the tracks. The machine-gunners seemed to start firing all at the same time.

We waded in the muck, almost impossible to move. We tried to reach up for our ammo and guns.

I tried to untie the radio, holding my rifle between my legs. The radio wouldn't come. Silence, and *then* the enemy RPG fire resumed. Our own return fire stopped as everyone ducked and sweated. Men were shouting. Running.

The paddy was deep. It was dark brown and green, and we struggled in it. The tracks started to back up. It was, we learned later, the standard maneuver when they take RPG fire, they go into reverse, full speed.

They ran over us. There was no way to move, as in a nightmare when your legs are filled with concrete and not attached by nerves to your brain.

The tracks ran over Paige, taking away his foot. One of the lieutenants was hit, but he went to pull Paige out of the mud. Ortez was cushioned by the muck when a track went over him, but his leg was broken. He went stumbling past me, bloody and without his helmet or machine gun. He threw his canteen away, and his ammo belt. He stopped and turned and hopped away from a track, crying.

A track ran over a little guy named McElhaney. He couldn't move because he carried a radio, and he was smothered and crushed dead.

The tracks kept rolling backward. The gunners poured fire into the village. More grenades came rifling out into the paddy.

It was the battle at Bull Run, all of us churning to escape the vehicles. We threw ammo and helmets and belts into the paddy. Gear was strewn everywhere. I left my radio dangling from the track and tried to catch the company. We finally stopped. We formed a skirmish line along a paddy dike.

The tracks stopped in front of us.

Smith walked over and said he wanted to call headquarters and get an air strike on the village. He wiped off his glasses and chuckled. I went to the track and took off the radio, and a company RTO came along to pull his out of the paddy. Then the jets came in for twenty minutes.

We watched them drop napalm.

Medics gave Paige morphine as he sat inside one of the tracks. He smoked and didn't cry or smile, perfectly composed. He knew he was going back to the world; that was all that mattered. "Jesus, man, does it hurt? Christ, it must hurt like hell." Some of Paige's black friends were inside the track, talking to him and even laughing. "Man, you're a lucky sonofabitch. War's over."

"Shit, man, just smoke that weed. You got yourself a million-dollar wound there. Home tomorrow, no problem."

Smith poked his round head inside the track and told Paige to hold on, we had a dust-off on the way. When it came, I threw yellow smoke out into the paddy. The grenade fizzled smoke, then sank. Someone else tried red, the helicopter saw it, and we walked through a mudstorm, carrying Paige and Ortez and some others.

Then the tracks formed a straight line and moved out. We walked between and behind the monsters, looking for McElhaney. The mud came up to our knees, and the water was sometimes near the crotch, and we strutted like Fourth of July majorettes. But the steps were horrible to take. No one really wanted to be the man to find Mac. Captain Smith lagged behind. One of McElhaney's friends came over to bum a cigarette and then walked with me. He talked about the old days, when he and I and Mac were the new guys in the company.

"I never thought you'd make it this far," he told me. "An' I guess I never thought Mac would make it either. Me, shit, I'm going into Chu Lai and re-up, next chance I get. Christ, I'll give the army three years to get out of this shit. I ain't bullshittin', I'm gonna re-up, I don't give a damn. Can't take this shit anymore."

Up front somebody found McElhaney under two feet of water.

Most of the blood was out of him. He was little to begin with.

He was white and wet, and the algae were on him. Some men gingerly rolled him into a poncho. We leaned against a track and smoked, not watching.

Captain Smith joined us. He joked, he didn't smoke, he didn't help with McElhaney, and he asked what we thought about all this.

"Sir, I think we should just turn the tracks around and get away from these villages. That's my advice, sir."

"Well, Timmy boy, that's why I'm an officer. We've got our orders."

"Okay, sir. But if the ground commander thinks it's best to . . ."

Captain Smith jerked a finger into the air and did a comic double-take, acting, and he smiled like a fool, acting. "Right, Timmy boy. I almost forgot that. Maybe I'll talk to the track commander about yer idea. Thanks, Timmy boy!"

But the two officers argued and then decided to move into the hamlet. So Smith ordered the first platoon to move out of the paddy into a dry, wooded area, covering our left flank. Then he sent one squad from the third platoon onto the right flank—a broad, very large paddy dike, perhaps twenty feet wide.

The tracks started rolling, and the troops moved behind them very slowly. We picked up a machine gun and some rifles and ammo on the way. It was stuff we'd thrown away during the retreat. We went fifty meters.

Then someone in the squad on our right flank triggered a mine, a huge thing. I thought they were mortaring us. Smith was just in front of me, and he hollered "Incoming," and we both dived into the slime and sank into it.

Voices calling for medics started in small, bewildered, questioning tones, softly, afraid to say the word. Then we were all bellowing. A medic stumbled across the exposed paddy, running with high, fullback strides. He sank onto his knees and tried to help the dead ones until he saw they were dead. Other medics slowly came over. They were tired of putting their fingers into blood.

The tracks stopped and everyone waded to paddy dikes to sit down and wait. One of my friends walked over and showed me a two-inch hole in his canteen where sharpnel had hit.

"Not bad, huh?" Barney said. He was a very young soldier, and he was more amazed than frightened. He grinned. "Pretty lucky, there it is. I'll have some good stories to tell when the ol' freedom bird takes me home."

Captain Smith ambled over and sat down on the dike. "Got me a little scratch from that mine. Here, take a look. Got myself a Purple Heart." He showed me a hole in his shirt. It looked like a moth had done it, that small. "My first big operation, and I get a Purple Heart. Gonna be a long year, Timmy. But wow, I've lost a lot of men today."

Two Vietnamese scouts had been killed by the mine. When the dust-off choppers came in, we loaded up the dead scouts and eight wounded GI's. In half an hour Alpha had lost seventeen men.

After the helicopters had gone, Captain Smith and the track commander argued again. We sat on the paddy dikes, the enemy presumably still around, while the two officers debated issues of honor and competence. Smith said the track commander should have informed him that they had a policy of backing up when taking incoming fire. "Damn it, I'm going to suffer for this," Smith said. "What's my commander to think? He's gonna see a damn casualty list a mile long, and it's only my first operation. My career is in real jeopardy now." And the track commander swore and said Smith should have known the rudiments of track warfare. He muttered something about ROTC.

Then they argued about what to do next. Orders from battalion headquarters were clear: We were supposed to sweep through the hamlet to a helicopter pickup zone a few miles away. Finally the two officers decided to forget the sweep. The tracks turned around. We would make a wide skirt around the village, let the Viet Cong have the place.

We climbed aboard the tracks, keeping our gear on, and the column moved ten yards and stopped. The track commander radioed Captain Smith and said the infantry would have to get off and walk, taking the lead.

"You want us to walk, huh?" Smith shook his head. "Now, why the hell do you want us to *walk* three miles?"

"Mines," the track commander said. "This place is loaded with them. You'll have to put a man up front with the mine detector and have all the troops walk ahead of us to look for the damn things."

"My God, man, you want me to use my men to find mines for you? You *mean* that?"

"That's affirmative," the track commander radioed back. "The mines are pretty thick. We've got a mine detector, may as well use it."

"Mine detector, hell. That thing won't find a mine in a million years. Might as well tell my troops to roll along in front of your tracks to clear the way."

"Look, be reasonable. What's going to happen if

one of my tracks hit a booby-trapped 105? It'll blow us all to hell."

"Reasonable. You tell me to be reasonable? You're trying to tell me to use my men as mine detectors? What about the Bouncing Betties, damn it? One of my men hits a Betty and he's dead. Christ, those things don't even scratch a track."

Smith called his platoon leaders over, explained the problem, and tried to talk them into going along with the track commander. The platoon leaders laughed and said they wouldn't do it. Smith said he knew it was a crazy order, but what could he do? The platoon leaders walked away, ignoring him, but Smith told everyone to jump off the tracks. We lined up, ready to walk. When the platoon leaders sulked and delayed, Smith waddled over to the command track and continued the argument. In ten minutes he waded back and told us to get aboard. The track commander was tired of arguing, it was late in the day, and everyone was in a hurry to eat hot chow. We turned our backs on the village and rode away.

After this disaster, Captain Smith tried to regain his leadership, but the lieutenants gracefully avoided him. He was openly ridiculed by the men. There was half-serious talk about his being a marked man. The black soldiers hated him, claiming it was only a matter of time before someone chucked a grenade into his foxhole, and we were all careful not to sleep near Captain Smith.

His sense of direction was absurdly bad. We were late arriving at objectives. He was never certain where he was or where to go next. Calling for artillery rounds to mark the company's position, he would sometimes motion at a piece of the sky, predicting the round would burst there; then the explosion would come directly in back of him. He would chuckle and holler at his platoon leaders for getting him lost.

In mid-July we were CA'd into a burning village. Jets were dropping tons of napalm. There was a company of GI's on the opposite side, engaged with the enemy in loud, desperate-sounding battle, and we could hear their calls for dust-offs over the radio as we went down.

We landed and spread out and moved in on the ville. The first platoon was hit immediately. A grenade knocked off a lieutenant's left testicle. The gunfire was close and loud. Smith hollered at the third platoon, and they ran up and lay down and returned fire into a hedgerow. The fire fight lasted five minutes. Then the first platoon radio operator called. His friend was shot, he said. His platoon leader was mangled.

We called the battalion commander, a tough colonel circling around in his helicopter directing things. We asked him to come down to evacuate the wounded. The colonel asked if we had a secure landing zone, asked where the enemy was, asked if the dust-offs were urgent, and then said we should call into headquarters for a regular medivac chopper.

The first-platoon radio man broke in. "We've got two men badly hurt. Need an urgent—repeat, urgent —dust-off. One of the men will die. There's no time."

"Roger," the colonel said. His helicopter buzzed the treetops, scouting the battlefield. He flew for another five minutes, then called again and told us to call for a dust-off through the normal channels. "Damn it, I haven't got time to do everything. Got to direct this operation."

We acknowledged, but the first-platoon man broke

in and said his friend had a sucking chest wound and would die without quick help.

"Soldier, stay off this net. You relay your damn requests through your CO. Stay out of this."

"Roger that, sir." The first-platoon man paused, then came on the radio one more time and said his CO was unconscious and bleeding.

The jets pounded the village. With each pass, smoke ballooned into the air; then another jet whined over our heads, over the village, into the smoke; then more smoke shot up. We shouted over the noise, firing into the enemy's hedgerow, waiting for the dust-off.

When the jets went home and the smoke was gone, the battalion commander came down and picked up the wounded officer and a dead man with a sucking chest wound.

Later, we entered the village. There were two dead VC. An old lady wandered about, smiling, and that was all. We took papers off the VC, and the woman went away.

The men made a perimeter around the village. Since everyone knew we would be mortared, we dug our foxholes deep. And we set up listening posts inside the village itself. The place was full of tunnels and bomb shelters, and the napalm might have missed something.

In the night, the mortar barrage fell on us. Two men were wounded.

We slept some more.

Then Captain Smith and three others opened fire inside the perimeter. The thing they shot lay there all night, and in the morning we kicked a dead pig.

The next day we blew up tunnels and bomb shelters. A piece of clay came down and hit a man, slicing off his nose, and he drowned to death in his own blood. He had been eating ham and eggs out of a can.

That afternoon we continued through the countryside. We stopped and rested on a hill. Thinking about security, Captain Smith sent a patrol down to circle the hill—six men. There was an explosion a while later, and I called out to them, asking if everything were all right. They didn't answer, so we waited. Captain Smith said it was just a stray artillery round. We ate supper. Then a member of the patrol stumbled through the bushes, bleeding, sobbing. The patrol had hit a big mine. The rest were still down there. The medics sweated and tried, but two of the men were dead, and one lost his leg, and the others couldn't move. The battalion commander flew down and picked them up. He got a Distinguished Flying Cross for that, an important medal for colonels.

Near the end of July, Alpha Company was choppered to the top of a mountain. There was a monastery there, but intelligence told Captain Smith to look for a fight.

We landed next to a statue of the Buddha, and a monk strolled out to meet us. He brought watermelon and other fruit. So we went inside the gates and walked down neatly swept paths, through gardens and past small statues.

The monk held his head high on a neck he did not use. To look left or right, he pivoted his body at the trunk. He had a round, bald skull with brown skin stretched over it like cowhide tanning in the sun—skin pulled tight over the cranium and over a thin, pointed nose.

He pointed out his gardens with watermelons and things that looked like cucumbers. The paths were red-colored; the buildings were white and scrubbed. He showed us a brood of children, half of them orphans, he said, and the rest just abandoned. He pointed at his bald head and chuckled.

The place was as far from the war as you can get in Vietnam: south of Chu Lai, north of the Batangan, east of Highway One, west of the sea. It was on the side of a ridge line that sprouted palms and pine and, in his gardens, watermelon and fruit.

He showed us where to dig foxholes in his yard. With grace, he accepted C rations and allowed the medics to look after the children. Night came, and the monk went into a white building, burned incense, and went to sleep.

I kept guard, slept, took the guard again when it began to rain. I opened C rations in the darkness and listened to the radio. Someone called and reported movement on one of the mountain slopes. Out that way, GI's threw grenades at the breeze. They blew a Claymore mine, settling the matter for the moment. The Claymore gave an echo. Its steel pellets, seven hundred of them, went through the bushes, across the courtyard, where they blew bits of white stone from the Buddha's belly. He protested no more than the monk when we went away in the morning.

During the first days of August, Captain Smith was relieved of his command of Alpha Company.

XVIII

The Lagoon

Where a reef of scarlet coral touches against the Batangan Peninsula there is a lagoon rimmed by stretches of sand for a mile and more.

Beyond the salt water and beyond the sand there are growths of tropical fir and coconut trees, living sparsely off soil made more of clams and chloride than nitrogen. Farther inland come layers of sedge, paddies brewing rice and mosquitoes, swamps, clusters of jungle, verdant places where every sort of thing grows and decays.

First, though, is the lagoon, and it was there that Alpha Company made its camp. We came to protect the place. We came to provide security for the small village that took its food and living out of the lagoon. On a knob of land overlooking the village, we erected sunshades, dug foxholes, rolled out canisters of concertina wire, and made friendships with the villagers. The childern brought us crayfish, and we gave out C ration candy bars, a formality at first, but later the exchanges seemed something more than barter. We swam in the lagoon and did some fishing. We skipped rocks across calm waters. Sometimes we walked about the beaches without our rifles.

The lagoon must always have been a good place. Plenty of fish from the sea, cool winds for land that is always hot. Protection from the reef. In the old days, centuries ago, the lagoon must have been a port for travel and adventure. Who knows, perhaps the place once boasted its own lagoon monster, a sea serpent with green scales and bulging eyes and an appetite for careless fishermen and little boys.

It sets a fellow to thinking. Back when kings were kings and tyrants were called tyrants, the lagoon must have had a proud populace.

On the red reef they would have built large fires at night to keep it clear of shipwrecks. The people would have been naked on the hot days. They would have had white pagodas for Buddha, they would have burned sticks of incense in his honor. For the boys, adulthood would have meant bringing in fish from the sea.

The place would have been tranquil, even with a lagoon monster lurking about.

But all that is conjecture, and it is better to describe the lagoon as Alpha Company found it.

On each black midnight a hundred fishermen take a hundred bark skiffs down to the lagoon. They sail a half-mile into the lagoon, each boat lighted by a single lantern, a hundred white lights bobbing among the waves. It looks like Minneapolis when you come in at 15,000 feet on the midnight 707 from Seattle. The fishermen fish until morning. Then they bring in eel, octopus, squid, red snappers, crayfish, and seaweed.

Old men arise just at daybreak and go down to the water to greet the fishermen.

The old men wade out and help push the boats to the sand; then the fishermen sleep, and the old men lay out the catch to dry and smoke in the sun.

In an hour the women come out, the old men go to sit in the shade, the children do some sweeping.

It is not a village Gauguin would have painted; it is not a romantic place. The village starts where the coral meets land, and it extends for two hundred meters along the beach. It is a war village, a refugee camp.

It is made of army tin. The huts are long, metal barracks, one contiguous to the next, identical in squalor, crammed full of families, surrounded by rows of the new kind of army concertina wire, the sort with tiny razor blades replacing barbs. Two thousand people live there.

Beyond the wire are mines. The curved stretch of sand holds Bouncing Betties. The ground is loose, and the Betties pop into the air, explode, and spray sand and clams and flesh out for twenty yards. The beach is littered with Bouncing Betties. And where there are no Betties there are booby-trapped grenades, some set out by the enemy, others scattered by the Popular Forces to defend the village.

Where the fir and coconut trees grow, the ground is firmer. There, along with Betties, are M-14 toe-poppers, booby-trapped artillery rounds, and other gadgets. The lagoon is not the place you would have found if you'd explored the place with Magellan or Captain Cook or whoever sailed here in other centuries.

Still, when it is midnight and the fishermen are out on the water, the lagoon is calm, and it's as good a place to be as any. And when a full moon is out, it is the best place to be. Village guards beat out "all is well" on hollowed hunks of wood. The breeze blows in, you can see the moon shining a beacon across the water, tracing a path out to the boats. On those nights you can think about how the lagoon once was. You may have met a lover there.

It was hot. I was sleeping when the boats came in, but when Bates and I went down to the water we saw the catch was tremendous. Thousands of baby shrimp lay drying on the beach. Two children were pulling seaweed out of the nets. Silently, the old men were brushing black, smelly pitch onto the skiffs, preparing them for another night on the lagoon. A jumble of women were leveling sand for a village square. Already they had raised a flagpole, and on top of it was a yellow flag crossed by horizontal red stripes, the South Vietnamese flag, looking grotesque, out of place.

In the middle of the morning the women were well into their work and the fishermen at the third level of sleep. I was at the radios. We were called by one of our patrols along the beach: "It's a mine. We'll need a chopper out here, urgent. Guy's whole leg is gone, have to make it fast. Got our position?"

I made the old frantic call to headquarters, curious about who I was trying to save, names and faces flicking past, a list of wanted posters. "Bandit 99, this is Zulu 10. Request urgent dust-off. U.S. soldier, mine, he's hurt bad. Grid 789765."

"72, this is 10. Need to know extent of injuries. Any hostile fire. You got a secure landing zone? Got smoke?"

A new lieutenant was out with the patrol, and he was cool. "Well, I don't know, the guy's hurt real bad, it's his whole leg, he's just lying there. We'll make some kind of litter, just get that bird out here. No enemy fire, no problem. LZ secure, we're standing by with smoke."

165

The dust-off was completed in eighteen minutes, but it wasn't fast enough. The soldier had stepped on a rigged mortar round, and there wasn't a chance.

He was a quiet, intelligent Texan, an NCO named Martin, but when the chopper lifted him off the beach and over the old lagoon, he died.

The next day, July 7, Bates and I cooked crayfish at dusk. Resupply had brought us canned margarine and lemons, and it turned out to be a real feast. In the morning we called in another dust-off. A GI named Peterson had gone fishing with hand grenades, and one of them blew his belly away. Six of the men carried him out of the lagoon. They had him in a poncho. The plastic was filled with seawater and Peterson's stomach.

At Landing Zone Minuteman, an American fire base half a mile from the lagoon, mortarmen perform a nightly ritual, week after week. Acting as the village's line of light-artillery protection, they calibrate their weapons, determine grid coordinates for defensive firing, and, finally, they register the guns for accuracy by firing upon uninhabited target areas around the lagoon. If the lagoon is attacked, they're able to fire immediately.

One night they made a mistake. A buck sergeant determined the gun elevation and deflection and called the numbers to his RTO, who passed the information on to a gun crew. The firing data recorded in the gun pits were not the data recorded in the bunker. At 10:20 P.M. the guns fired, the same old ritual, and at 10:21 the rounds were falling on the lagoon's little village.

Thirty-three villagers were wounded. Thirteen were killed: Bi Thi Cu, 2 years old; Dao Van Cu, Bi's brother, 4; Le Xi, 2; Dao Thi Thuong, 9; Pham Thi Ku, 4; Pham Khanh, 15; Le Chuc, 8; Le Thi Tam, 10— the children.

Dust-off helicopters shuttled to the lagoon all night, working in the rain, ferrying the casualties to hospitals and morgues. GI's scrambled through the rain and tin rubble for survivors. Military inspectors were there within an hour, taking notes and looking grim.

A month later, when the reports were finalized and guilt apportioned, solatium payments were made to the families of those killed and maimed—twenty dollars for each wounded villager; thirty-three dollars and ninety cents for each death. Certain blood for uncertain reasons. No lagoon monster ever terrorized like this.

XIX

Dulce et Decorum

Tim:

How does one respond to such a letter as that?
July was always a hot month, sweaty kids running
through the streets with sparklers, but where are
they now, tell me? With you, I fear; some of them
still shrilly laughing—crazy patriots.

I suppose if we gain anything from this un-
sought experience it will be an appreciation for
honesty—frankness on the part of our politicians,
our friends, our loves, ourselves. No more liars
in public places. (And the bed and the bar are,
in their way, as public as the floor of Congress.)

For honesty has become something wholly other
than childhood innocence or adult aspiration.
Rather, because there is no time, no cause or
reason, for anything but truth, honesty has become
fundamental to life itself. We must be honest or
be silent.

And especially for you, living in your terrible
private world, mercilessly made public to death, I
try to be honest. I am in Vietnam, but I am not in
combat, and I'm sometimes conscious enough to
be grateful for that. Having sought the answer
to why we are both here and finding none, I now
ask why you are out there, doing the battling,

and not me. Again, no answer. Would I willingly risk those few moments again at Fort Lewis, when two decisions were made that fated two lives? Would I risk the chance to persuade you to enlist for an extra year to avoid the infantry for the possibility that you might have persuaded me not to? And would I now be there beside you, or instead of you? The whole thought of wishing for the chance over again is just as absurd as the actual act.

How far into this must we go to find meaning? Here, I want desperately to help you. To give you a ticket to a place I know in Norway. And there is nothing, absolutely nothing, I can do but encourage you to be honest, as you have been.

But here I am in Long Binh, this sprawling, tarred, barbed-wired sanctuary for well-bred brass and well-connected lifers. What they are doing to win or end the war, I don't know. As for my own contribution to military history, I spent the first month in Asia as a legal clerk, helping the army to chastise its pot smokers and non-conforming, often futilely proud black soldiers.

At night, I spend time on guard or waiting on standby alert. There's no reality to it. Long Binh is not the war; it's not really part of Vietnam, not with all the cement and Pepsi-Cola and RCA television sets. One night last week I watched a spectacular fire fight—gunships sending down red sheets of metal—then there was a long silence, a gap of blackness, before the sound of the gunships reached me, just a buzz. I imagined you out there. I'm only an observer, Tim, audience to a tragic Fourth of July celebration.

Erik

A new man, another southerner, took charge of Alpha Company in early August. He had been in command for only an hour when he marched the men into a mine field. Then the dust-off helicopters were there, taking away a dead man named Rodriguez and a cripple named Martinez. They were Spanish-American, bewildered companions. They'd spent time together snapping Kodak pictures of each other in gallant, machine-gun-toting poses.

But when all that happened, I was in Chu Lai, looking for a new job. Captain Smith, probably feeling guilty for having copped out on a long-standing promise for a job sorting mail in the rear, had given me a three-day pass and a wry grin. He wished me luck. I hitchhiked around the sands of Chu Lai, showing off letters of recommendation from Captain Johansen and Alpha's first sergeant, trying to talk someone into taking me on. But the army has plenty of mediocre typists. I couldn't change a tire, and no one wants a tired grunt anyway. There were no offers, and I rejoined Alpha Company.

If foot soldiers in Vietnam have a single obsession, it's the gnawing, tantalizing hope of being assigned to a job in the rear. Anything to yank a man out of the field—loading helicopters or burning trash or washing the colonel's laundry.

Unlike the dreamy, faraway thoughts about returning alive to the World, the GI's thinking about a rear job is not dominated by any distant, unreachable, unrealistic passion. It's right there, within grasp. You watch the lucky ones wade into a rice paddy and toss their packs into a chopper. They grin and give you the peace sign. There is a self-pity, an envious loneliness, when they are gone.

GI's use a thousand strategies to get into the rear.

170

Some men simply shoot themselves in the feet or fingers, careful to mash only an inch or so of bone.

Some men manufacture ailments, hoping to spend time in the rear, hoping to line up something.

And one man maintained a running record of the dates when rear-echelon troopers were due to rotate back to the world. When one of those days came near, he'd send back a request for the man's job.

But the best route to a rear job, the only reliable way, is to burrow your nose gently up an officer's ass. Preferably the company commander. If an officer takes a fancy to you—if he thinks you're one of his own breed—then you're a candidate for salvation. But you've got to spill over with clear-headedness; you've got to bleed with courage, morbid humor, unquestioning forbearance.

For the soul brothers, that route is not easy. To begin with, the officer corps is dominated by white men; the corps of foot soldiers, common grunts, is disproportionately black. On top of that are all the old elements of racial tension—fears, hates, suspicions. And on top of that is the very pure fact that life is at stake. Not property or a decent job or social acceptance. It's a matter of staying alive.

With either the hunch or the reality that white officers favor white grunts in handing out the rear jobs, many blacks react as any sane man would. They sulk. They talk back, get angry, loaf, play sick, smoke dope. They group together and laugh and say shit to the system.

And this feeds the problem. Pointing at malingering and insubordination by the blacks, the officers are free to pass out jobs to white men. Then the whole cycle goes for another round, getting worse.

For Alpha Company, the phenomenon finally hit a

171

point when the cycle was spinning so fast, with such centrifugality, that it blew apart.

Alpha's first sergeant was hated by the blacks. Rear assignments, they said, were going to ol' whitey, and they intended to do something about it. "Damn first sergeant's responsible," they said. "He's the Man, we'll get him."

When we lost four men one day, the first sergeant saddled up and took a chopper out to join us until replacements came in. He was a tall, even-handed man. He seemed to hate Vietnam as much as anyone. His National Guard unit had been activated, and he'd been torn away from his town and friends, same as the rest of us, by politics and circumstance. We were mortared the night he arrived. He crawled on his hands and knees with everyone else. To be fair, the first sergeant may not have been a leader, but he was quiet and helpful enough.

In the morning we began searching villages, moving through two or three of them. We moved across a broad paddy. The company was formed in a long, widely spaced column. The first sergeant, probably to show us he had guts and could take charge, walked up front with the company commander and the RTO's, and we moved slowly.

I was watching the first sergeant. He lurched backward, and dirt and a cloud of red smoke sprayed up around his thighs. He stood and gaped at the short explosion. He didn't say anything. As if he were trying to back out of the shrapnel and noise, he took three steps. Then his legs disintegrated under him, and he fell heavily on his back.

It exploded right under him. No one felt any particular loss when the helicopter landed and we packed him aboard.

That evening we dug foxholes and cooked C rations over heat tabs. The night was hot, so instead of sleeping right away, I sat with a black friend and helped him pull his watch. He told me that one of the black guys had taken care of the first sergeant. It was an M-79 round, off a grenade launcher. Although the shot was meant only to scare the top sergeant, the blacks weren't crying, he said. He put his arm around me and said that's how to treat whitey when it comes down to it.

In two weeks, a black first sergeant came to Alpha.

Except for one or two of them, the men in Alpha Company were quietly, flippantly desperate for a rear job. The desperation was there all the time. Walking along under the sun, pulling watch at night, waiting for resupply, writing love letters—we thought and talked about all the rear jobs waiting back there. We were not all cowards. But we were not committed, not resigned, to having to win a war.

"Christ, you *know* I'll take anything they give me," Barney said. "I'll shovel shit for 'em during the daytime and drink me some beer nighttime, no problem. They send me to Chu Lai, and I'll stack bodies at the morgue. I'll toss bodies and bloody shit around and just drink it in, they give me the job. There it is."

And Bates and I would pull radio watch together some nights. "When Chip and Tom got it—that damn mine—that did it for me. Nam was some kind of nervous game till they got blown up. I wasn't even there then. Jesus, I was just listening over the radio. But, damn it, that did it. I knew those guys. I'll take my job back there, anything."

So along with the rest of Alpha Company, I followed the new commander during August, hoping for a rear-echelon assignment and trying inconspicuously to avoid death. It seemed odd. We weren't the old soldiers of World War II. No valor to squander for things like country or honor or military objectives. All the courage in August was the kind you dredge up when you awaken in the morning, knowing it will be a bad day. Horace's old do-or-die aphorism—"Dulce et decorum est pro patria mori"—was just an epitaph for the insane.

Alpha spent most of August on top of a stubby, flat hill to the north of Pinkville. It was an old corn field, a dusty and hot place without trees. We ran patrols during the days. At night we were mortared. It was a sort of ritual. The sun went down, we ate, smoked a little, played some word games, and at about ten P.M. the mortar rounds came in.

It was hard to keep a decent foxhole in that corn field, the soil was so chalky. The sides simply caved in on you. In the end, we dug narrow sleeping trenches and just lay there, half-asleep and sometimes talking to one another, wondering when the barrages would stop.

The whole thing was so well coordinated and timed that we learned to urinate in the first hour after sunset so as not to be standing when the explosions started. No one was hurt during the nightly sessions, but it was frustrating. Looking down into the paddies, we could see the red flashes of the mortar tubes, we could hear the ploop of the rounds shooting out.

They would spray our hill with 82mm rounds for twenty seconds, then pack up and go home. We would call for gunships and send our own mortar fire on them, but it was always too late. It was better to turn in the trenches and go to sleep.

Despite the ten-o'clock attacks and all the heat and dust on the little hill, the month of August was not bad. No one was killed. Few were seriously hurt. Sunstroke and blisters, nothing worse. It was God's gift. We would lie there at night, listening to metal tearing through the hedgerows and shrubbery; in the morning we would find impact craters only yards from our sleeping holes.

Resupply choppers brought in hot meals daily. We guzzled cases of iced beer and sodas. Morale was high —we were in a bad place, but no one was being mangled, and we were blessed. Nothing could go wrong. On one early-morning patrol, we chased two Viet Cong into a bunker. The company commander and a lieutenant threw in grenades and emptied magazines of M-16 ammo into the hole. They threw in more grenades and fired more bullets. The bunker seethed with smoke. The Viet Cong threw out a rifle. Some GI's went down and pulled them out. One—a young, riddled boy—was dead. The other was older, barely alive. Blood oozed from torn, rust-colored flesh where the shrapnel hit. He pleaded with the scout to save his life. Our medics tried to patch him, but it was clear he would die. We began cutting down a tree to allow space for a medevac chopper. Then the man died. We left him sprawled there; chickens were pecking at the dust around him when we went away.

Back at our corn field, the scout went through the older Viet Cong's papers. "That VC—he VC district chief," he said. "Big man. Mean bastard."

"No shit?" the company commander said. He grinned. "Hey, we got ourselves a VC district chief. Killed a VC honcho back there."

The company commander was elated. He called battalion headquarters and gave the news. We stayed up late that evening, talking over the kills, congratulating ourselves for being tough, stealthy, lethal soldiers.

But, when it got late, we quieted down, and everyone admitted it was coincidence and fortune. And, of course, at ten P.M. we were mortared.

Near the end of August, helicopters carried Alpha Company to another hill, this one alongside the South China Sea. A refugee camp was being built there, and our job was to watch civilians clear the land and put up huts. Although the place was less than a mile from our corn field, we were not mortared—only an occasional sniper—and it turned into a vacation. We sent out one patrol. A mine-sniffing dog went along. The dog stepped on a mine, and it blew his trainer's foot away.

It was there beside the ocean that I got my rear job. They wanted a typist in battalion headquarters; they wanted me. I dug a six-foot-deep foxhole that night, and I slept in it. In the morning Barney came to wake me and said I was a lucky son of a bitch. We went to the sea and swam, ducked some sniper bullets on the way, and I threw my gear into a helicopter, and it was done.

XX

Another War

In the rear area, protected from the war by rows of bunkers and rolls of barbed wire, I rejoined the real United States Army.

Thanksgiving: The first demarcation point, a roadside marking post. It drizzled, the start of the monsoon season. LZ Gator was turned into a gray hill of mud. The mess hall served up a surprisingly toothsome meal of turkey, dressing, two kinds of potatoes, cranberries, pies, mixed nuts. Like a family dinner. Men plodded in from the bunker line, gorged themselves, and stood by the stoves to dry off, then tramped on back to the wire. The FNG's, fresh from the Combat Center in Chu Lai, served the food and obeyed us like good FNG's must. "More, FNG, more!" A tentative smile, a look over at the mess sergeant, then the FNG's dipped in and gave us more.

The daily life: I worked in S-1, battalion headquarters. According to someone's administrative chart, S-1 was the brains of the battalion, the nerve center or some other such metaphor. But the description was inaccurate. We were bureaucracy, no more or less, albeit a miniature bureaucracy. We processed the FNG's when they came into the battalion. We processed dead people, too, taking casualty reports, keeping logs of how and when and where they died. We processed and

177

processed. Mail. Requests for transfer. R & R applications, applications for leave. We dispensed awards—Purple Hearts, one and the same for a dead man or a man with a scraped fingernail; Bronze Stars for valor, mostly for officers who knew how to lobby. And we gave out penalties, processing courts-martial and reprimands and other such business.

Dull. But the boredom and routine were painless, something like jumping out of a frying pan and into a sort of steam bath, not a fire. I thought about Martin Ross, the gung-ho marine who wrote with such fervor about his Korean War days, about his preference for the front lines over the rear areas. Though I could understand his distaste for monotony, it struck me as a major triumph of heroism to give up monotony for its horrible opposite. So I made the best of it, churning out the paperwork like a man who loves his job, making myself indispensable.

Christmas Eve: An office party, Kodak cameras snapping posed pictures to drool over when we get old, a grand feeling of friendship. The adjutant, a young and likable captain, led us in the drinking. The re-up NCO told dirty jokes and war stories, and we laughed at them all. The mail clerk was there. And the casualties clerk, the legal clerk, the awards clerk, the administrative NCO.

Out on the bunker line the men shot up flares and threw hand grenades into the wire, celebrating the occasion, whatever it was. At midnight sharp, the sky over LZ Gator erupted. Star clusters, flares, illumination rounds from the fire base's mortar tubes. We all went outside to watch. Afterward the re-up NCO and a grizzly master sergeant decided to teach me how to shoot craps, and at 4:30 on Christmas morning they went away muttering about beginner's luck, the old story. I spent the money on a new tape recorder–radio set.

Christmas Day: Duplication of Thanksgiving—drizzling rain, another good meal. We ate while the chaplain played Christmas music over a set of loudspeakers attached to the chapel. Bing Crosby's "Silent Night," the Johnny Mann Singers' "Oh, Come All Ye Faithful." It was a working day, by administrative fiat. But in battalion headquarters we arranged the day in shifts, one man in the office at all times, a bottle of excellent PX Scotch as a companion.

At midday, the captain sent two of us into Chu Lai, only an eight-mile ride, to pick up enough booze to last through the night. We found the liquor, caught a glimpse of Bob Hope trying to be funny in the rain; then we drove back to the fire base. Around ten o'clock that night everyone straggled into the headquarters building, nothing else to do, and we drank away Christmas, talking about how bad it would be if Charlie decided to attack that night, a good chuckle.

Now and then, to help slice the monotony into endurable segments, floor shows came to LZ Gator. Korean girls, Australian girls, Japanese girls, Philippine girls, all doing the songs and routines and teases that must be taught to them in some giant convention hall in Las Vegas. It was all the same, but variety didn't mean much. Each show started with one of those unrecognizable acid-rock songs, faded off into "I Want to Go Home—Oh, How I Want to Go Home," then a medley of oldies-and-still-goodies, none of them very good. Then some humor, then—thank God, at last—the stripper.

The black soldiers would arrive an hour before show time, cameras poised for a shot of flesh, taking the front-row seats. The white guys didn't like that much. A few whites tried arriving even earlier, but, for the next floor show, the black soldiers were ready and waiting two full hours before curtains-up. The colonel, a married man, slipped into the floor show about halfway through, as if coming just to see how things were going, just checking up. But he was not late for the finale.

Everyone drank. Most of us drank in excess, but the colonel would kill one beer and stop there.

Then the climax came. The men, roaring drunk and with tears in their eyes, would plead with the stripper—beg her, bribe her—to finish the job. But nothing ever came of it. We went away exhausted.

"Jesus," Bates moaned, sitting down behind his typewriter, dripping with sweat. "Jesus, this isn't healthy." He vowed never to watch a stripper again, not unless it was a personal, command performance. Near the end of our tours, Bates and I stopped going to floor shows altogether.

Nights: If you have no friends, if you don't know the right officers, if you're unlucky, you pull bunker guard. You stare into the wire, the same hunk of hillside, night after night. But if you work in battalion headquarters, you're home free. You spend your nights in the office, sleeping on a cot or reading or writing letters or writing a book. You're there to answer the telephone, but no one calls. Unless it's a casualty report. In which case you jot down the man's name, his serial number, the extent of injuries, the grid coordinates, the hospital he's been taken to. For a moment, just as you hang up the phone, you remember. But you go to sleep again, or return to your book. Or you just sit in the office and listen. The sounds at night are different on a fire base than in the field. There's rhythm to the sounds. Artillery fire booms out across the hill, huge guns firing in support of the field companies. Mortar tubes pop out illumination rounds over the fire base, lighting things up for the bunker guards. It all disturbs your sleep sometimes, and you find yourself cursing the guns, forgetting and ignoring how they helped you once upon a time, long ago, back in the old days when you were a soldier.

LZ Gator was attacked only once while I finished out my tour. Sappers were inside the wire before anyone knew it. With perfect cunning, perfect timing, they slipped in, blew up a pile of ammunition, killed a man, hurt some others. In the morning, we combed the hill. Altogether, six dead Viet Cong. Some officers loaded them into a truck and drove them down to a village at the foot of LZ Gator and dumped them in the village square.

R & R: Like going home. Sydney, Australia. Buddy Greco sang songs for me in the lounge of Sydney's Chevron Hotel: *once upon a time, very long ago*. You know the atmosphere? Dark club, girls strewn about like so many loose flower petals. Greco's sweet, slow, caressing music, backed by muted trumpet and sax and piano and crystal champagne glasses. I had a girl with me. The R & R Center lined her up when I arrived. I got off the plane, listened to a lecture on decorum, then went to a row of desks where old ladies sat with huge card files full of eager Australian girls.

An old woman picked out a name and dialed the number: "Hello, Sally? This is Hilda de Grand, here at the R & R Center. I have a nice young man here, he'd like to know if you're busy this evening? No? Yes? Oh, yes. A nice, handsome young man. Yes, black hair, just as you had down on your card. Here, I'll put him on."

"Hi, Sally."

"How do you do."

"Fine. Thanks." I forgot how to do it. "I, uh, just got in. From Vietnam." This is ridiculous. Doesn't she know?

"Oh, how nice."

"Yes."

"And do you like Sydney? Beautiful city, don't you think?"

"It's great. Anything is great, you know." Anything. She could look like a dachshund.

"I suppose so. All the boys say Vietnam is a positively ghastly place."

"Ghastly."

"You're a soldier? Some are navy people."

"Army."

"Well, you'll like Sydney."

"Haven't seen much of it yet. Actually, all I've really seen is the R & R Center. And the airport. The weather's nice."

"Chilly—terribly chilly for this time of year." The pause, a cue.

"Well, perhaps we can warm it up together." Starting to get back in the groove, a long time away.

"Fine, perhaps we can." She didn't laugh, but she didn't back away either. "What do you have in mind?"

"Oh, I don't know." It didn't seem possible. What did she think I had in mind, for Christ's sake? But I was civilized, I remembered that. "Buddy Greco? Dinner. Drinks."

Sally turned out to be nice. Buddy Greco, though, was superb. The club—all the warm feelings, the cordialities—was better.

I didn't fall in love. I spent most of my time alone, searching out the libraries, hitting bars at night, going to the ocean once. Then, for the last night, I visited the old ladies again and celebrated my departure with a girl named Frances.

After R & R, Vietnam was no longer even an adventure. Returning from R & R was something like walking out of one of the floor shows. Sweating, drained, blood boiling. Then back to the second-class war of the rear area.

After a long lapse in our correspondence, I began writing to Erik again. His tour in Vietnam was nearly over:

> I'll be taking a flight, that phoenix we both dream of, and I keep thinking how proper it would be for us to take it together. Leaving this land is an experience to be shared. But, for now, I wait, as you too must be waiting. Along with waiting, however, I try to keep a certain perspective—my old perspective as a watcher of things—and what I see lately is no good. This morning, coming out of the hooch, I watched as a junior officer literally kicked a Vietnamese woman out of the company area adjacent to ours. I watched. The observer, the peeping tom of this army. Doing nothing. I was suddenly sickened by the thought of the near two thousand years that separate my life and that of a Roman centurion who stood by a narrow alley leading to Golgotha and who also watched, doing nothing.
>
> What difference then? What earthly change have centuries of suffering and joy wrought? Is it only that Christ is become a yellow-skinned harlot, a Sunday-morning short-time girl?
>
> Needless to say, I am uncomfortable in my

thoughts today. Perhaps it's that I know I will leave this place alive and I need to suffer for that. But, more likely, what I see is evil.

With letters and Scotch whisky and with a comfortable but confining blanket of rear-area security, I settled down to wait.

XXI

Hearts and Minds

The Chieu Hoi, a scout for Charlie Company, came into the headquarters building. He stood in a corner and waited for a captain to notice him. Then he said: "Sir, my baby is sick. She is in Tam Ky, twenty miles from here. I must have a pass for three days to see her."

The captain said: "Is your baby sick now? I wonder. Or are you afraid to go to the field with Charlie Company tomorrow? How come your baby gets sick just when Charlie Company's going to the field?"

Quietly and unassured, the Chieu Hoi persisted: "Sick."

The captain pushed back in his chair, tilting it onto its back legs. "Look, you're a valuable man for us. You've got knowledge we GI's haven't got—all about mines and booby traps, how to find the stuff without blowing a leg off. Right? A guy like you can spot ambushes in time to save some lives. You're needed out there. You're getting paid to go to the field tomorrow, not to run away on pass."

Abashed, the Chieu Hoi said: "Not so. The baby is sick. The doctor—"

"See here," the captain said, stern and fed up. "What do I do when *my* baby gets sick? Hell, my wife and kid are thousands of miles away. The kid gets sick, and my wife takes him to a doctor, simple as that. Or she goes down to the drugstore, buys some pills. Nothing to it. That's how things work. But I don't skip out on the first plane if I hear the kid's got a high temperature."

The Chieu Hoi said: "Not many good doctors here. Wife is afraid."

"Now, damn it," the captain said, "this here's *your* goddamn war. I'm here to fight it with you and to help you, and I'll do it. But you've got to sacrifice too. Tell me how this war's gonna be won with you and others like you running off when things get tight? How? Hell, you're an ex-VC, you know how they think, where they hide. If I come over here and bust my balls, well, shouldn't you take the shit with everyone else?"

The Chieu Hoi said: "You are here for one year. I've been in war for many billion years. Many billion years to go." He was embarrassed, not quite distraught. He turned to look for help from others in the office. A fellow's pride will suffer when he pleads for favor. A fellow suffers when he is a suspect coward.

"Now, listen here, I want to help you, really," the captain said. "But I'm a soldier, so are you, so's everyone around this place. Sacrifice—it's the name of the game. Why not just go down to Charlie Company and saddle up for the field. Have a beer or two, your kid will make it."

"Baby very sick, maybe die. My wife is afraid."

"Well, the soldiers down at Charlie, they're afraid too. Maybe you can save some of them. You ain't gonna save the baby."

"They don't like me, the people in Charlie Company."

186

"Well, now it comes out. How come? There must be a reason?"

"I'm Chieu Hoi, old VC."

"Shit, you save their asses, and they'll fall in love with you," the captain said. "Look, if you do a job and help out, they'll like you just fine. Get their respect, and no sweat. Charlie Company will like you just fine. And your kid will be okay too."

The Chieu Hoi mumbled "Never happen," and he succumbed. He left by the front door, and it wasn't a day before he was AWOL.

XXII

Courage Is a
Certain Kind of Preserving

"So a city is also courageous by a part of itself, thanks to that part's having in it a power that through everything will preserve the opinion about which things are terrible—that they are the same ones and of the same sort as those the law-giver transmitted in the education. Or don't you call that courage?"

"I didn't quite understand what you said," he said. "Say it again."

"I mean," I said, "that courage is a certain kind of preserving."

"Just what sort of preserving?"

"The preserving of the opinion produced by law through education about what—and what sort of thing—is terrible . . ."

PLATO, *The Republic*
Book IV, 429b–429c

Major Callicles looked like an ex-light-heavyweight champ. He had a head like a flattened 105 round, a thick, brown neck, bristling stalks of hair, bloodshot eyes, a disdain for pansies. He was the battalion executive officer—second in command. He bragged that he'd started out as an NCO, thrived on the discipline, and gone on to become an officer, avoiding West Point and doing it the hard way.

Barrel-chested—staves and beer and all—he was a last but defiant champion of single-minded, hard-boiled militarism. He listed his hates in precise order —moustaches, prostitution, pot, and sideburns. And since all four were either tacitly or explicitly permitted in Vietnam, he harbored a necessarily silent hate for the new, insidious liberality infecting his army.

Moustaches, while authorized by new regulations, were quickly outlawed. It was rumored he carried a dull and bloody razor to be used on even a wisp of overnight hair.

Next was prostitution. It was an all-consuming outrage. A whorehouse flourished at the very foot of LZ Gator, the battalion fire base, and he muttered he would get rid of it.

He pursued pot and sideburns like an FBI agent; he prosecuted violators with inquisitorial zeal.

"Guts," he would mutter. "This army needs guts. GI Joe's turned into a pansy. O'Brien, you show me a soldier with guts, and you can have this job." He hunched his shoulders, stood stiff-legged, held a cigarette like a pencil, and turned to look at me out of one eye, scowling and squinting.

Three months after Major Callicles took charge, *Time* and *Newsweek* and every other scrap of paper blowing into Vietnam heralded the My Lai massacre.

The massacre happened in March of 1968. That was one year before I'd arrived in Vietnam; over a year and a half before Callicles took over the executive officer's job; long before our battalion had taken over the Pinkville–My Lai area of operations from Lieu-tenant Calley's Eleventh Brigade. But Major Callicles stuffed the burden of My Lai into his own soul. He

189

lost sleep. He lost interest in pot and prostitutes, and his thick, brown face became lined with red veins hemorrhaging with the pain of My Lai. Like the best defense attorney, he assumed the burden of defending and justifying and denying—all in one broad, contradictory stroke.

At first he blamed the press: "Christ, those rags—you don't really believe that crap? Jesus, wake up, O'Brien! You got to learn the economics of this thing. These goddamn slick rags got to sell their crap, right? So they just add together the two big things in this hippie culture: People like scandal and people hate the military, not knowing what's good for them. It's knee jerk. So they look around and choose My Lai 4—hell, it happened over a year ago, it's dead—and they crank up their yellow journalism machine; they sell a million *Times* and *Newsweeks* and the advertisers kick in and the army's the loser—everybody else is salivating and collecting dollars."

But for Callicles it was more than an outrage, it was a direct and personal blow. "Christ, O'Brien, I'm one of hundreds of executive officers in the Nam. This battalion is one of hundreds. And they got to pick on us. There's a billion stinking My Lai 4's, and they put the finger on us."

When Reuters, AP, CBS, ABC, UPI, and NBC flew in, Callicles took them into his little office and repeated the same grimacing, one-bloodshot-eye-in-the-face, shotgun argument he perfected with us privately. "Look, I thought the press was supposed to be *liberal—liberal*. Maybe I'm no liberal, but I know something about it. I never went to college, but I can read, and I know the press isn't supposed to try a man in print. That's what we got juries for, you know, they do the trying, it's the law. That's *liberal*, isn't it? Just be quiet one minute—isn't that what the liberals say? You don't insinuate guilt until you're in the courthouse and everyone's got evidence ready and there's a judge and a jury and a court reporter to take it all down."

A reporter said they were just printing the allegations of other soldiers, former GI's.

"Hell, you don't believe *them*? Some pipsqueak squeals, and everyone runs to make a national scandal. We're trying to win a war here, and, Jesus, what the hell do you think war is? Don't you think some civilians get killed? You ever been to My Lai? Well, I'll tell you, those *civilians—you* call them civilians— they kill American GI's. They plant mines and spy and snipe and kill us. Sure, you all print color pictures of dead little boys, but the live ones—take pictures of the live ones digging holes for mines."

A reporter asked if there isn't a distinction between killing people you know to be the enemy and slaying one hundred people when no one is shooting and when you can't distinguish the mine-planters from the innocent.

"Now, look here, damn it, the distinction is between war and peace," Callicles said. "This here is war. You know about war? What you do is kill. The bomber pilot fries some civilians—he doesn't see it maybe, but he damn well knows it. Sure, so he just flies out and drops his load and flies back, gets a beer, and sees a movie.

"Just answer this: Where's the war in which civilians come out on top? Show me one. You can't, and the reason is that war's brutal—civilians just suffer through it. They're like unarmed soldiers—they're dumb and they die; they're smart, they run, they hide, then they live." Callicles pushed the words like moist worms through his teeth.

A reporter asked if there isn't a distinction between the unintentional slaying of civilians from the air, when there's no way to discriminate, and the willful shooting of individual human beings—one by one, person to person, five yards away, taking *aim* at a ditch full of unarmed, desperate people.

Callicles snorted and told the reporter to ask the dead people about the distinction.

Maybe the dead people don't see the difference, the reporter said, but what about the law. Shouldn't guilt have something to do with intentionality?

"Come on," Callicles said. "I'll take you on out there. You judge for yourself. This is a war, and My Lai is where the enemy lives—you can see for yourself."

Major Callicles herded groups of reporters out to My Lai 4, flying them over the hamlet and giving them a peek at the dank, evil-looking place: white mounds showing the gravesites; a cluster of huts that seem to have been there a thousand years, identical in squalor and with a kind of permanence that makes them just a fixture of the land; utterly lifeless; thick, dark green splotches where the land is low; yellow-brown craters where artillery rounds have hit. Even in stark mid-morning daylight the place looks a monotonous gray from the air. Your eyes can stay on the place for only seconds; then you look away to the east, where the sea is so much more appealing.

The My Lai scandal did not go away. Major Callicles was charged with heading a task force to secure the village and prepare the way for General Peers, Lieutenant Calley, and the investigative team. He attacked the job of blowing mines and marking out safe paths and digging defensive positions. Haunted by what he was doing, he began to drink heavier than ever, his eyes shifted from detail to detail, searching out stability in his world; other times he glared into dead space.

The investigation ended, and Major Callicles was awarded a letter of commendation. But he read it and gave a sly grin and tossed it into a pile of wastepaper. He spent more time than anyone at the officers' club on LZ Gator, playing poker—winning and losing big pots of military currency—and drinking. Afterward he came down to his office and debated with us.

"What do people want when they send men to fight out there?" he would ask, growling.

"To search out and destroy the enemy."

"Yeah, yeah, I know that. But what do they want when the enemy is ten years old and has big tits—women and children, you know. What then? What if *they're* the enemy?"

"Well, you kill them or you capture them. But you only do that when they're engaged in combat, sir. It's a civil war, in part, and even if some of them come down from North Vietnam, they look like the South Vietnamese. So you've got to assume—"

"Assume, bullshit! When you go into My Lai you assume the *worst*. When you go into My Lai, shit, you know—you assume—that they're all VC. Ol' Charlie with big tits and nice innocent, childlike eyes. Damn it, they're all VC, you should know that. You might own a diploma, for Christ's sake, but does that mean you can't trust your own eyes and not some lousy book? You've been there, for Christ's sake!"

"But, sir, the law says killing civilians is wrong. We're taught that, even by the army, for God's sake."

"Of course killing civilians is wrong. But those so-called civilians are killers. Female warriors. Poppa-san out in the paddy spying."

"But with that philosophy, you'd have to waste all

193

the civilians in Vietnam, everyone. I mean, how do you know when this Poppa-san or that Poppa-san is VC? They look alike. They all dress in black pajamas and work in the paddies and sell us Cokes. Hell, we might as well go down into Nouc Mau, the little village down by the gate, and just kill them all."

"That's ridiculous. You're exaggerating the argument."

"Reductio ad absurdum. Logical extension, sir."

"Bullshit! Nouc Mau sure as hell isn't My Lai 4, you know that. It isn't a goddamn mine field; kids in Nouc Mau don't go around setting up booby traps and spying on us."

"Now, that's quite an assumption. Who knows? The whole town might be VC. We'd be the last to know it. But the point is, sir, we can't say that those two-year-old kids were planting mines out at My Lai. Can't prove that *all* those dead women were spying on Lieutenant Calley. Go ahead, how do you prove it? Or don't you have to?"

"Look here," Callicles said, "can't you see we're over here trying to win a war? Is that so goddamn hard to understand, just trying to win a war and go home? I want to go home, you want to go home, General Abrams wants to get his ass back to the world. But, Jesus, with the communists doing things like at Hue—killing and doing extortion, stealing rice and taxing the shit out of everyone, when they're *living* in Pinkville—really living there, eating and sleeping and making mines—Christ, then you got to go after them. Show me a war . . ."

With the My Lai investigation complete, Major Callicles turned back to whores and dope smokers and malingerers, apparently with the hope of turning the army back toward World War II professionalism. "Professionalism," at least, was the word he used most. But what he wanted and what he furiously went after was a return to the old order. Callicles's suspicion and assumption, in the end, was that the massacre at My Lai may have in fact happened just as *Newsweek* reported it, but that dope and whores and long hair—all suggesting the collapse of discipline—were responsible. It conflicted with his other arguments, of course, but it was his belief. So he crusaded.

He assigned officers and NCO's to the fire base's gates, and every jeep entering LZ Gator was searched for marihuana. Sometimes he stood out in the rain, spending hours peering into gas tanks and under seat cushions. "You don't smoke dope, do you, troop?"

"No, sir!"

"You'd tell me if there's dope in this vehicle, right?"

"Yes, sir!"

"Okay. But I'll check, just to make sure some goddamn VC didn't sneak some dope onto this vehicle. Get out."

Long lines, sometimes stretching out fifty yards, waited while Major Callicles did his duty.

At night he would roam the fire base. He would check the perimeter bunkers and the barracks, go to the officers' club and drink and gamble, and make another round.

One evening a medic shot himself in the foot. He'd been scheduled to go to the field the next day, and it was fair to guess it had been intentional. His friends carried him into the medic's hootch and laid him out, and in thirty seconds Major Callicles was there.

"You bastard, Tully, you goddamn coward, you shot your ass, didn't you, you dirty, sneaky little shit. You're a coward. Well, goddamn it, you little shit, I'm reading your goddamn rights to you right now while you're busy bleeding the pus and shit out, and you'd better tell me you understand what's going on." He snapped out a book and read Tully's rights to silence and attorney and jammed the book back into his pocket and leaned over the table and glared into Tully's face. "All right, you fuckin' coward, you understand? I'm gonna question you while you're bleedin' an' you don't have to answer, but you sure as hell better answer, understand?"

"I understand," Tully whined. The medics were cutting off his boot.

"Goddamn it, Tully, you know who the hell you're talkin' to, goddamn it, you little shit? This is Major Callicles, an' you call Major Callicles 'Sir,' you understand?"

"Yes, sir, Jesus, it hurts, sir!"

"Shit, I'd like to bite the bloody little stump! What the fuck you expect, you little shit? You shoot yourself, you point an M-16 and blow off your toe 'cause you're afraid to go out there and help guys getting shot up by Charlie, an' you bitch 'cause it hurts. Aw, it hurts! Shit. Okay, Tully. Now, did you shoot yourself? You shot your goddamn self, didn't you?"

"God, it hurts! I was just cleaning it. It hurts, Jesus, sir, I'd just—"

"Cleaning, cleaning, cleaning, bullcrap!" Callicles put his nose down into Tully's face, and Tully tried to turn his head to the side, but Callicles leaned more and kept his mouth against Tully's nose. "You were scared shitless you'd get blown away out there, right? So you thought what the hell's a toe, an' you blew it away, an' now you're going to the world and sit in a hospital and read some comic books and drink some beer, right? Bullshit! Tully, bullshit! You're gonna get a court-martial, that's all you're getting."

"Accident, sir." He moaned, choked.

"Accident?"

"Yes, I don't—"

"You sneaky little shit! You trying to lie to a major, you little coward asshole?"

Back in his office, Major Callicles talked about courage: "You know, O'Brien, when it comes down to it, people like me are lifers because we've got to show that there are still people with courage around in this world." He smiled and wrinkled his nose, then dropped into a mean stare. "It's the old story. Guts to stand up for what's right. Sure, it's almost futile—like the last man walking around after the bomb, just to show there's still people around, but it's still something to be proud about. You kids make me feel like an old man. I'm forty-four, I'm like an old man in the army. But I don't care what the new culture says, young people like you are wrong when it comes to guts. You know what courage is? I can tell you that. It's not standing around passively hoping for things to happen right; it's going out and being tough and sharp-thinkin' and *making* things happen right."

He grabbed his helmet, leaving the problem of what is right unresolved, and went on up to the officers' club.

Some of us sat about and talked about Major Callicles. Bates took the position he was outright crazy, and Porter agreed in essence, but he admired the man's pizzazz. "The way he grimaces, they don't make them that way anymore! Nazi Germany turned out some good ones, of course. Remember Himmler: Ja wohl, was ist richtich ist richtich! To the fore, to the fore, we'll not surrender; save the Motherland; sorry— Save der Vaterland! Really, he's got character, we need men like Callicles."

"He's nuts," Bates muttered, and shined his boots.

"Of course he's nuts. That's the beauty of the man. But put him in Himmler's shoes! Try him out that way. Can't you see it? Stuff a monocle into one of those eyes. Isn't it great? *Sieg heil!*"

"No, he's pathetic. That man will hurt somebody, wait and see."

Porter had a way of affecting seriousness. "Oh, no. Hold on for a second. You've got to appreciate style, Bates, you've got to use some imagination. Now, just think: Major Callicles is now Wehrmeister Hintenberg. Guten Tag, Herr Hintenberg, how goes das war, gut? Ach, ja! Aber die Menschen—pot, die fräulein, das Haar. Going to pot!"

"Cut it out," Bates said. "Sometimes I like the guy."

At midnight Major Callicles came down from the officers' club, eyeballs rolling. "O'Brien! Get your pack and rifle and ammo and a radio. We're goin' on down to Tri Binh 4—run a little patrol, just you and me and a Vietnamese scout. Let's see if you got guts."

I said I was on duty.

"Duty, shit! Who the hell's running this battalion? Saddle up, let's go."

"You serious, sir? Come on . . ."

"Damn straight, I'm serious. Good to get out in the field. Scared?"

I said I was plenty scared.

"Good," he said, winking at one of the other men. "Good soldiers are always scared; that way they don't get careless and shit in their pants when the action starts. Maybe we'll get some kills, surprise everybody, huh? Ol' Major Callicles goes out and gets Charles, and everyone else's back here puffin' on the weed an' lookin' at skin flicks, an' old Callicles, the ol' soldier's out there messing up Charles. We'll have people shittin' in their pants tomorrow, let's go."

I laughed and looked at some paperwork. He went into his office, and Bates was saying what a close call that was when Major Callicles came out in his armored vest and told me to get my ass into a helmet.

We drove out of the perimeter and picked up a Vietnamese scout in Nouc Mau. Then we drove down Highway One toward Tri Binh 1.

A squad from Delta Company was there to meet us. Callicles smoked a cigarette and asked for the best route to Tri Binh 4. The squad leader pointed out across a paddy and advised him not to go, that the VC liked the place. But Callicles was spinning around in booze and courage, and he told me to turn on the radio, and we waded out into the paddy.

Callicles took the point. The scout was behind him, then me and the radio, and a man from Delta took the rear.

It was a half-hour hike. We roamed around the outskirts of the village until Callicles found a trail to ambush.

"Okay, put up a Claymore," he said, much too loudly, teasing. "Let's see if you really pulled that field duty. Sure you can do it."

He crawled with me up to the trail and leaned over my shoulder. I put the thing in.

"Shit, O'Brien, you wanna kill groundhogs? We're after VC, not fuckin' groundhogs, for Christ's sake." He was talking too loud, too much. The scout crawled up and asked what was wrong. "Shit, O'Brien's on a goddamn groundhog hunt, for Christ's sake. He's trying to kill fuckin' groundhogs." The scout asked who O'Brien was, and Callicles laughed and clunked me

199

on the rear. "This soldier, right here. College grad. Good man, though, even if he can't set up a Claymore. You got guts, O'Brien, shit, I knew it anyhow. Here, let me get that thing in, and we'll get some kills."

He pointed the Claymore up at the sky, and I asked if he were hunting eagles, but he growled and crawled off the trail and left the thing as it was, useless.

"Okay, now we wait. You have to be quiet, dead quiet. I'll start any shooting, you just wait and follow my lead. Don't forget to blow the damn Claymore."

Major Callicles lay on his belly and was quiet. Rain sprinkled down, but it was a comfortable, gentle rain, reassuring because the VC were no more willing to venture out in it than GI's.

Callicles didn't stir for an hour. The man from Delta rolled over and asked if Callicles was stoned. I said yes, and he giggled and shook his head and rolled away.

In a few minutes the man from Delta Company rolled back and pointed toward Major Callicles. "Jesus, either he's asleep or dead. Look, he's got his head all cradled up, he hasn't budged."

Callicles was ten yards away, flat on his stomach, but it was too dark to make out his face.

"Hell, my mama told me to watch the booze, sweet woman. Should I throw a rock over there?" He thought about it and decided he'd just be shot dead, and he rolled away.

In an hour Callicles stood straight up and walked to the Claymore, walked down the trail, and peered into the village. "Shit, O'Brien, there ain't no goddamn VC in Tri Binh 4." He called it out like a drill sergeant hollering at a training company. "Who says Tri Binh 4 is such a bad place; you guys been giving me a line of bullshit? Jesus! Yank out that firing device and let's beat feet out of here." He stalked away like a prince, talking to himself: "Jesus, and I thought Tri Binh 4 was bad shit! Think I'll hold a goddamn party here tomorrow night, everyone can waltz and drink punch, for Christ's sake. Shit, a damn lark, a breeze, like walking through a patch of Maryland daisies!"

In the morning the battalion commander rebuked Major Callicles. Things were tense, but afterward the major paced around his office, grinning and winking at everyone. "All it takes is guts—right, O'Brien?" Several nights later he burned down the whorehouse, and the next day he was given two hours to leave LZ Gator for good. It hurt him, leaving.

XXIII

Don't I Know You?

The air is still, warm. Just at dusk, only the brightest stars are out. The Southern Cross is only partly there.

A man rolls a gate open and you walk carefully onto a sheet of tar. You go up eighteen steps.

The airplane smells and feels artificial. The stewardess, her carefree smile and boredom flickering like bad lighting, doesn't understand. It's enraging, because you sense she doesn't want to understand.

The plane smells antiseptic. The green, tweedy seats are low-cost comfort, nothing at all like sleeping in real comfort on top of the biggest hill in the world, having finally climbed it. Too easy. There is no joy in leaving. Nothing to savor with your eyes or heart.

When the plane leaves the ground, you join everyone in a ritualistic shout, trying to squeeze whatever drama you can out of leaving Vietnam.

But the effort makes the drama artificial. You try to manufacture your own drama, remembering how you promised to savor the departure. You keep to yourself. It's the same, precisely the same, as the arrival: a horde of strangers spewing their emotions and wanting you to share with them.

The stewardess comes through the cabin, spraying a mist of invisible sterility into the pressurized, scrubbed, filtered, temperature-controlled air, killing mosquitoes and unknown diseases, protecting herself and America from Asian evils, cleansing us all forever.

The stewardess is a stranger. No Hermes, no guide to anything. She is not even a peeping tom. She is as carefree and beautiful and sublime as a junior-high girl friend.

Her hair is blond; they must allow only blonds on Vietnam departures—blond, blue-eyed, long-legged, medium-to-huge-breasted women. It's to say we did well, America loves us, it's over, here's what you missed, but here's what it was good for: my girl friend was blond and blue-eyed and long-legged, quiet and assured, and she spoke good English. The stewardess doesn't do anything but spray and smile, smiling while she sprays us clean, spraying while she smiles us back to home. Question. Do the coffins get sprayed? Does she care if I don't want to be sterilized, would she stop?

You hope there will be time for a last look at the earth. You take a chance and try the window. Part of a wing, a red light on the end of it. The window reflects the cabin's glare. You can't even see darkness down below, not even a shadow of the earth, not even a skyline. The earth, with its little villages and bad, criss-crossed fields of rice paddy and red clay, deserts you. It's the earth you want to say good-bye to. The soldiers never knew you. You never knew the Vietnamese people. But the earth, you could turn a spadeful of it, see its dryness and the tint of red, and dig out enough of it so as to lie in the hole at night, and that much of Vietnam you would know. Certain whole pieces of the land you would know, something like a farmer knows his own earth and his neighbor's. You know where the bad, dangerous parts are, and the sandy and safe places by the sea. You know where the mines are and will be for a century, until the earth swallows and disarms them. Whole patches of land. Around My Khe and My Lai. Like a friend's face.

The stewardess serves a meal and passes out magazines. The plane lands in Japan and takes on fuel. Then you fly straight on to Seattle. What kind of war is it that begins and ends this way, with a pretty girl, cushioned seats, and magazines?

You add things up. You lost a friend to the war, and you gained a friend. You compromised one principle and fulfilled another. You learned, as old men tell it in front of the courthouse, that war is not all bad; it may not make a man of you, but it teaches you that manhood is not something to scoff; some stories of valor are true; dead bodies are heavy, and it's better not to touch them; fear is paralysis, but it is better to be afraid than to move out to die, all limbs functioning and heart thumping and charging and having your chest torn open for all the work; you have to pick the times not to be afraid, but when you are afraid you must hide it to save respect and reputation. You learned that the old men had lives of their own and that they valued them enough to try not to lose them; anyone can die in a war if he tries.

You land at an air force base outside Seattle. The army feeds you a steak diner. A permanent sign in the mess hall says "Welcome Home, Returnees." "Returnees" is an army word, a word no one else would use. You sign your name for the dinner, one to a man.

Then you sign your name to other papers, processing your way out of the army, signing anything in sight, dodging out of your last haircut.

You say the Pledge of Allegiance, even that, and you leave the army in a taxicab.

The flight to Minnesota in March takes you over disappearing snow. The rivers you see below are partly frozen over. Black chunks of corn fields peer out of the old snow. The sky you fly in is gray and dead. Over Montana and North Dakota, looking down, you can't see a sign of life.

And over Minnesota you fly into an empty, unknowing, uncaring, purified, permanent stillness. Down below, the snow is heavy, there are patterns of old corn fields, there are some roads. In return for all your terror, the prairies stretch out, arrogantly unchanged.

At six in the morning, the plane banks for the last time and straightens out and descends. When the no-smoking lights come on, you go into the back of the plane. You take off your uniform. You roll it into a ball and stuff it into your suitcase and put on a sweater and blue jeans. You smile at yourself in the mirror. You grin, beginning to know you're happy. Much as you hate it, you don't have civilian shoes, but no one will notice. It's impossible to go home barefoot.